MW01714121

Credit Risk Management

GARP | Global Association of Risk Professionals

Second edition published in the United States of America by the Global Association of Risk Professionals

111 Town Square Place, 14th Floor
Jersey City, NJ, 07310, USA
Tel: +1 201.719.7210 • Fax: +1 201.222.5022

2nd Floor, Bengal Wing
9A Devonshire Square
London EC2M 4YN, UK
Tel: +44 (0) 20 7397 9630 • Fax: +44 (0) 20 7626 9300
Website: www.garp.org

ISBN: 978-1-933861-04-3

Printed in the United States of America

This book is dedicated to GARP's Board of Trustees,
without whose support and dedication
to developing the profession of risk management
this book would not have been necessary or possible,
and to the Association's volunteers, representing thousands
of organizations around the globe, who work on
committees and share practical experiences in numerous
global forums and in other ways, and whose goal is
to create a culture of risk awareness.

Contents

Introduction

The global financial crisis of 2007-2009 has made financial institutions even more aware of their responsibility for managing risks. In the wake of the spectacular, unprecedented, and fundamental transformation of the global financial infrastructure that has followed the crisis, the responsibility of risk managers has changed. At financial institutions worldwide, banks and regulators increasingly rely on the skills, knowledge, and integrity of risk managers to pilot the transforming financial system with improved risk management policies, practices, and systems.

As risk management has moved to the forefront of banking, risk managers are becoming increasingly visible, important, and trusted at banks. This evolution is driven both by banks themselves and by bank supervisors. Banks are increasingly sensitive to the role of risk management in making decisions. Supervisors have come to recognize that better understanding of risk management principles and practices is vital, not only for the success of individual banks, but also for the safety and soundness of the global financial infrastructure.

As a result, bank supervisors have refined regulations that were outlined by the Basel Committee on Banking Supervision in the International Convergence of Capital Measurement and Capital Standards, also known as the Basel II Accord. The changes to Basel II, and new regulations that form the Basel III Accord, reflect the new financial world order, codifying the risk management practices of many highly regarded banks. While this book does not specifically address the Basel II or Basel III Accords, it does reflect the principles and practices—both qualitative and quantitative—that they embrace.

Credit Risk Management is part of the GARP Financial Risk and Regulation (FRR) series that offers a qualitative introduction to banking risks, risk management, and the international risk-based regulation of banks. The goal of Credit Risk Management and other related volumes in this series is to ensure that the reader develops a deep understanding of the qualitative aspects of a typical large bank's risk management activities, including risk assessment, measurement, modeling, and management, across the trading and banking books.

Taken as a whole, the GARP FRR Series—Market Risk Management, Credit Risk Management, Operational Risk Management, and Asset and

Liability Risk Managements—enhances the understanding of specific risks and shows the right questions to ask when qualitatively analyzing the risks of financial instruments or assets. These books create a broad understanding of the key risks banks face and how these risks can be best managed.

Understanding the specific sources of risks is essential in the management process of measuring, monitoring, and managing risk. The material is presented in a user-friendly format enabling readers to understand the key qualitative risk factors and how they drive bank risk management. Each book contains numerous examples of actual financial events, as well as case studies, diagrams, and tables that explain these complex relationships. Overall, these volumes foster a better understanding of why and how financial risks emerge and how these risks can impact individual financial assets, financial institutions, financial systems, and ultimately, the global financial infrastructure.

Students who successfully complete market, credit, operational, and asset and liability risk management readings will gain a broad understanding of how the various risks reinforce each other. Such students are strongly encouraged to sit for GARP's International Certificate in Financial Risk and Regulation, an integrated look at the chief risks financial institutions face and how to best manage them. To complete the program, students may decide to take a certification exam.

These readings contain several technical terms used in banking and risk management. While the material requires a fundamental understanding of finance and banking, the intended readers are not practicing risk managers but bankers who want to have a better understanding of the qualitative factors affecting risks and who have familiarity with fundamental banking and finance concepts. This study text has adopted the standard codes used by banks throughout the world to identify currencies for the purposes of trading, settlement, and the displaying of market prices. The codes, set by the International Organization for Standardization (ISO), avoid the confusion that could result from many currencies having similar names. For example, the text uses USD for the US dollar, GBP for the British pound, EUR for the euro, and JPY for the Japanese yen.

Acknowledgements

Credit Risk Management, a volume in the GARP Financial Risk and Regulation series, has been developed, and now revised, under the auspices of the Banking Risk and Regulation Committee at GARP who guided and reviewed the work of the contributing authors.

The Committee would like to thank David C. Shimko, Ph.D., Peter Went, Ph.D., Amanda Neff, Graeme Skelly, Christian Thornæs, Andrew Cunningham and other members of GARP for their contributions to this latest edition.

Introduction to Credit Risk Management

Credit Risk Management, a volume in The GARP FRR Series, focuses on credit risk and credit risk management practices at global financial institutions. It consists of four interrelated chapters: the first chapter focuses on credit risk and the governance of credit risk management. The chapter also demonstrates a structure for credit analysis, the underwriting process and procedure for loan pricing. Use of credit risk models and an overview of expected and unexpected loan losses are also covered.

The second chapter describes some of the retail credit products; lending to SMEs; corporates; sovereigns and counterparty risk.

The third chapter discusses credit risk portfolio management, the use of models and methods of credit risk reporting. It also considers the review of the loan book, analysis of risk rating methodology and the process of stress testing under various macro and micro economic scenarios.

The final chapter looks at the regulatory view of credit risk capital requirements, evolution of the various Basel Accords and credit risk rating approaches and testing. It concludes with an overview of US agency guidance on leveraged lending.

CHAPTER 1

Credit Risk Assessment

Credit risk – performance with obligations
market risk – change value Traded sec

The four chapters of this book focus on credit risks. Chapter 1 focuses on credit risk and the governance of credit risk management, while Chapter 2 analyzes the risk of various credit products. Chapter 3 discusses credit risk portfolio management and, finally, Chapter 4 analyzes the regulatory view of credit risk capital requirements.

This chapter assumes prior exposure to basic credit analysis and focuses on a credit risk assessment framework that is used to value credit-linked obligations, such as loans, bonds, and lines of credit, as well as assessing the risk of those obligations. Building on this basis, the chapter addresses credit and its governance—including credit policies and governance of credit within a bank—before moving to analyze the core risk concerns in the credit assessment process for both bonds and loans. It is important to recognize that the credit risk terminology used in this module relates to all classes of credit risk listed above.

On completion of this chapter the reader will have an improved understanding of:

- The differences between credit and market risk. Credit risk is a form of performance risk in a contractual relationship whereas market risk derives from changes in the value of traded securities or contracts held by a bank. There is also a difference in time horizon: market risk is typically measured over short time periods (daily), credit risk is typically measured over longer periods (annually).

- The assessment of the credit risk of an issue or an issuer, and the need for credit losses to be quantified. A pricing model for credit reveals the factors that drive credit risk measurement: probability of default (PD), recovery rate (RR), exposure at default (EAD), expected loss (EL), loss given default (LGD), unexpected loss (UL), duration (D), and spread (S).
- The importance of credit policy and procedures to support credit risk management. At the core of credit risk management is a well-crafted loan policy that addresses credit risk considerations and is ratified by the bank's senior management or board.
- The practical application of a credit risk assessment framework, translating basic concepts of credit risk management into inputs to credit models.

1.1 Distinguishing Credit Risk from Market Risk

For most bankers, credit risk is much more important than market risk. These are bankers who focus much more on traditional lending and credit, and less on capital market activity. Understanding credit risk requires some familiarity with market risk, a topic outlined and discussed in *Market Risk Management*, another volume in the *GARP Financial Risk and Regulation Series*.

1.1.1 Credit Risk

The basic concepts for measuring credit risk—probability of default, recovery rate, exposure at default, expected loss, loss given default, and unexpected loss—are easy enough to understand and explain. However, even for those involved in risk management who agree on the concepts, it is not always easy to practically implement a method that is fully consistent with an original concept. Minor differences in how credit risk is estimated and measured can often result in large swings in estimates of credit risk, and big differences of opinion on how to proactively manage the credit risk. Such movements can have significant impacts on risk assessments and ultimately on business decisions (including the using of collateral, securitization, and credit risk mitigation).

The following sections describe some of the core principles of credit risk assessment, which are easily extrapolated to a wider range of credit risk assessment approaches ranging from straightforward consumer and retail credit products through sophisticated, multi-layered, structured commercial and institutional credit products to multi-borrower relationships that may contain corporate as well as sovereign credit risk.

Credit risk is a form of performance risk in a contractual relationship. In any contractual situation, performance risk refers to the possibility that one party in the contract will not honor its obligations to the other. Credit risk is usually defined as the performance risk associated with a financial contract (e.g., a loan, bond, or derivative contract). Hence, the potential failure of a manufacturer to honor a warranty might be called performance risk, whereas the potential failure of a borrower to make good on its payment requirements—both the repayment of the amount borrowed, the principal, and the contractual interest payments—would be called credit risk. A borrower or an obligor is defined as any party to a contract that has to perform a financial obligation.

Credit risk and default risk are used interchangeably (often the term credit event is used to describe default). Commonly used terminology in the financial markets, such as the ISDA master agreements, ascribe an array of actions that can impact the probability of repayment as a credit event, such as bankruptcy, failure to pay, loan restructuring or repudiation, loan moratorium, and accelerated loan payments.

Typically, credit risk resides in those investments that the bank has made in its banking book (loans and certain bonds that the bank holds until maturity, with no intention of selling to other banks). But there is also a credit risk that is inherent to trading: counterparty credit risk.

As counterparty credit risk relates to the trading activities of banks, it is the risk that the counterparty to financial instruments and over-the-counter traded contracts will default prior to the expiration of the contract by not making all contractually required payments. Financial instruments and contracts traded on exchanges are exposed to minimal counterparty credit risk, because of the exchange's clearinghouse, which assumes the risk of non-performance.

What distinguishes counterparty credit risk from traditional credit risk is the bilateral nature of this risk (i.e., the default of one counterparty can trigger a series of defaults with other counterparties which may only be indirectly related to the first defaulting counterparty). Moreover, due to the dynamic nature of trading and pricing, the exposures of financial instruments and contracts can change, and thus further complicate the assessment and quantification of the exposure.

1.1.2 Differentiating between Credit and Market Risk

In some cases, it is easy to distinguish credit risk from market risk. For example, a USD 100 loan collateralized with USD 200 in marketable securities such as equity has limited market risk, but an uncollateralized obligation to pay an amount linked to the long-term performance of the Nikkei 225 Index (an index that measures the performance of the leading Japanese stocks on the Tokyo Stock Exchange) has more inherent market risk than credit risk. Despite the overlap between market risk and credit risk, most banks have separate departments to evaluate these two risks, and make special provisions to deal with products that have both market and credit risk. In this chapter, we treat these two risks separately, understanding that a bank will strive to measure its total risk, which includes both market and credit risk in all its products and trading activities.

Credit risk differs from market risk due to obligor behavior. For a discussion of this, see Section 4.7 of Foundations of Financial Risk on The Credit Process and the five "C's" of Credit: Capital, Capacity, Conditions, Collateral, and Character. Sometimes obligors fail to perform because they deliberately choose to (lack of character), and sometimes they fail because they become unable to (lack of capacity). Sometimes, behavior is particular to a specific obligor (e.g., a company defaults on its debt because of the death of its founder), while other times, obligors fail because of overwhelming macroeconomic influences, such as the global financial crisis of 2007-9.

Both credit risk models and market risk models use historical data, forward-looking models, and behavioral models to assess risks. All of these models can be captured in a general credit risk assessment framework, which is explained in Section 1.2.

In some cases, credit risk is broader than the risk of non-performance in a contractual setting as mentioned above. Publicly traded issues, such as bonds and traded loans rated by credit rating agencies, may fall in value due to worsening credit conditions attributable to either the specific issuer or the economy as a whole. Worsening conditions increase the required yield spread above the risk-free rate, which in turn adversely impacts the value of the issue. This is different from the impact of lowering the security's credit rating, and is often called credit migration risk (which has evolved as an integral part of credit risk).

Risk quantification also affects the spread charged on credit products. As credit quality changes, so will the required interest rate and the price of the credit product. Spread risk captures the effect of price changes as investors' required return changes in anticipation of deteriorating market or economic conditions.

It is also important to emphasize the differences in time horizon: while market risk is typically measured over very short time periods (daily), credit risk is typically measured over a long time horizon (annually).

1.1.3 Estimating Credit Losses

For most bankers, the most familiar risk metric will be the adequacy of general and specific loan loss provisions and the size of the general and specific loan loss reserve in relation to the total exposures of the bank. The allowance for loan losses creates a cushion of credit losses in the bank's credit portfolio and is primarily intended to absorb the bank's expected loan losses, as determined by management following established credit policy guidelines, which are enacted by the bank's board of directors in accordance with supervisory and regulatory input.

Historically these decisions were made on a case-by-case basis, but with the growing sophistication and automation of lending, as well as the increasing complexity of credit products, computationally complex products have standardized the credit assessment and evaluation of individual retail and commercial borrowers. Furthermore, the introduction of bankwide credit risk software accelerated in response to the Basel II Accord, as regulators recognized the need for improved analysis and oversight of the risk assessment process, particularly for more complex credit products. Under the terms of the Accord, banks can qualify to use their own internal expected and unexpected loan loss models to determine their regulatory capital requirements.

In Chapters 2-4 of *Market Risk Management*, a book in the *GARP Financial Risk and Regulation Series*, pricing models are used to identify risk drivers in FX, interest rate, equity, and commodity products and positions. The same strategy is followed here: a pricing model for credit reveals the factors that drive credit risk measurement.

- PD (Probability of Default): the likelihood that the obligor or borrower will fail to make full and timely repayment of its financial obligations over a given time horizon (duration)
- LGD (Loss Given Default): the amount of the loss if there is a default, expressed as a percentage of the exposure's value
- EAD (Exposure At Default): the expected exposure at the time of default

- EL (Expected Loss): the average expected credit loss over a given time period
- UL (Unexpected Loss): the loss in excess of expected loss
- RR (Recovery Rate): the proportion of the EAD the bank recovers
- D (Duration): duration to default
- S (Spread): spread for pricing credit-linked obligations

In addition to measuring the credit risk of an individual exposure, and computing the credit risk and potential credit losses of a credit portfolio, credit concentration risk should also be considered when pricing credit.

The first four factors are consistent with the names in the Basel II Accord's framework. Those four credit risk factors have different drivers depending on whether the credit obligation is considered as retail, Small and Medium-Sized Enterprise (SME), corporate, counterparty, or sovereign. (Counterparty credit risk is similar to corporate credit risk but differs in several important ways. Section 2.4 explains these differences.)

The extent of credit losses needs to be quantified to assess the credit risk of an issue or an issuer. Using the factors EAD, LGD, PD, EL, UL, and RR, the losses for the two different types of credit products (i.e., loans and bonds) can be measured.

The core difference between loans and bonds is in the way they are treated from a legal perspective. A loan is a contractual agreement that outlines the payment obligation from the borrower to the bank. The loan contract is designed to cement the relationship between one borrower and one or more lenders. While the bank or group of banks may have the right to assign a loan to another party, the intention is that the loan will reside in the bank's banking book or credit portfolio. This is known as "keeping the loan on the books." Typically, a loan may be secured with either collateral or payment guarantees to ensure a reliable source of secondary repayment in case the borrower defaults. Also, loans are often written with covenants that require the loan to be repaid immediately if certain adverse conditions arise, such as a drop in the borrower's income or capital. Notwithstanding an original intention of "keeping the loan on the books," the loan may be sold to another bank or an entity such as a fixed income fund that invests in loans.

By contrast, a bond is a publicly traded security. The structure is an agreement between the borrower (issuer) and the lenders (purchasers). Typically, bonds are held in the trading book of the bank. In some cases bonds may be assigned to the banking book if the bank intends to keep the bonds until maturity.

Collateral support, payment guarantees, or secondary sources of repayment may all support certain types of bonds, but there is also a wide range of bonds without these secondary sources of repayment. Such supports are considered structuring characteristics specific to each bond. In the case of default, a bond investor's potential recovery depends on the seniority of a bond, the collateral supporting the bond, as well as other transaction-specific conditions. Typically, it is the market and the investors in the bond that monitor the performance of the borrower (issuer of the bond) and of the bond.

The higher the seniority of the bond, the higher the likelihood the investor will receive the face value. Thus, an investor in a senior bond would expect to receive a larger share of the face value in default than an investor in a junior or subordinated bond. Similarly, quality of collateral support may impact the value of a loan or a bond; a potential change in the value of supporting collateral in liquidation is often termed recovery risk.

1.1.4 Expected Credit Losses

For all credit instruments, the expected loss can be determined by considering two outcomes: default and non-default. In the event of non-default, the credit loss to the bank is zero. In the event of default, the loss is the assumed fraction (LGD) of the exposure (EAD).

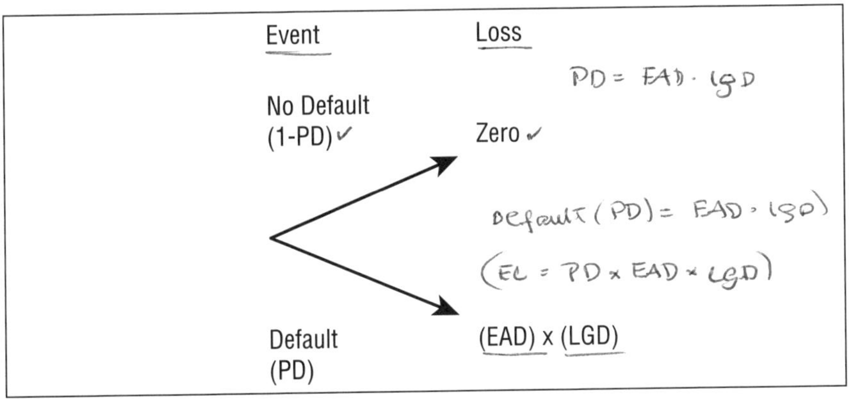

FIGURE 1.1 Expected Credit Losses

The expected loss is the probability-weighted average of the two outcomes above:

$$EL = PD \times LGD \times EAD.$$

EXAMPLE

Bank A makes a USD 100,000 loan to Company A, a retailer, at an 8% interest rate (paid annually), which has an annual expected default rate of 1.5%, a loss given default of 40%, and collateral (inventory) of USD 80,000. In this case, over the next year, the bank's EAD is 108,000 – 80,000 = 28,000 i.e., the loan value plus accrued interest minus collateral. The expected loss is 1.5% × 40% × 28,000 = 168. The assumption is that the collateral will not affect the LGD as a proportion of exposure. However, collateral does affect the EL: a similar bond without collateral would have an expected loss of USD 648 (=1.5% × 40% × 108,000).

While the concept of expected loss is straightforward, the calculations can be quite complex. For example, the assumption of a one-year expected loss on a multi-year loan would not be sensible for pricing purposes as expected losses would have to be extrapolated into the future to be able to price the loan.

1.1.5 Unexpected Credit Losses

Unexpected losses are losses in excess of the expected loss and are expressed at a certain statistical confidence level (i.e., the average total loss over and above the mean loss). Traditional Value-at-Risk (VaR) models use the statistical distribution properties of prices and returns on financial instruments to quantify the potential level of losses at a given confidence level for each instrument separately and, in case of a portfolio of instruments, in aggregate. As these approaches quantify a possible range of values, credit risk managers have adopted this statistical and quantitative approach to estimate and compute the potential range of future credit losses. While market risk measurement typically uses distributions that are relatively symmetric around the mean, credit risk measurement uses distributions that are skewed, as the likelihood of significant losses is lower than the likelihood of average losses or no losses.

These statistical estimates offer a range of losses around the expected loss for individual loans as well as for portfolios of loans. Collateral and strict underwriting standards can reduce the expected loss of one loan. In a loan portfolio, the aggregate expected loss captures the sum of the expected losses of the individual loan exposures. This loss cannot be diversified through active credit portfolio allocation decisions that are made to reduce the inherent loan concentrations. Rather, active loan portfolio management embracing diversification of exposures across industries and geographic areas can only reduce the variability of losses around the mean, and thus the range of unexpected losses.

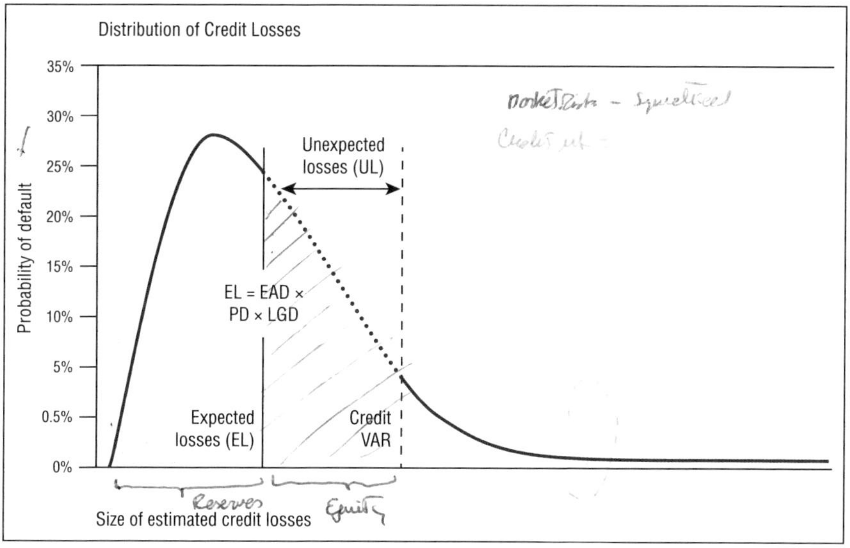

FIGURE 1.2 Expected and Unexpected Credit Losses

Reducing unexpected credit losses is one of the core challenges banks face. While expected credit losses are covered by loan loss reserves, as outlined in the following section, unexpected credit losses must be absorbed by the equity and capital of the bank: as shareholders benefit from unexpected returns, so shareholders must cover unexpected losses.

1.1.6 Expected Credit Losses and Loan Loss Reserves

Banks are expected to hold reserves against expected credit losses (a cost of doing business). At first, it would appear that bank reserves should be about equal to expected credit losses. Loan loss reserve calculations are determined by regulatory guidelines and the bank's internal policies. From a regulatory perspective, the loan loss reserves should cover quantifiable and likely losses, and not possible future losses.

To determine the right level of loan loss reserves, banks must be able to recognize problem loans in advance using effective loan review systems and other internal and external controls which identify, monitor, and manage asset quality problems in an accurate and timely manner. From a good management perspective, it is not the obvious problem loans—loans that demonstrate irregular payment patterns or are already delinquent—that cause difficulties, but rather loans where ongoing adverse developments are likely to affect the borrower.

These loan loss allowances are a general reserve for unconfirmed and yet-to-be realized losses. However, actual and realized losses should be charged off as soon as they are identified. Collateral levels and values may change (particularly when using financial instruments as a loan support), so banks are strongly motivated to recognize and charge off any confirmed credit losses. Where repayment support is not available through collateral or guarantees (due to either shortfall or unsecured lending), an early charge-off may capture the loss levels, which can be potentially mitigated by the outcome of bankruptcy or protracted delinquency processes.

In practice however, bank reserves differ from expected losses, and normally exceed expected losses for at least five reasons:

1. Time horizon
2. Look-back period
3. Unfunded commitments
4. Expected versus incurred risk
5. Charge-offs versus economic loss

With respect to the time horizon, EL is calculated over one-year periods because it is the standard established for Basel II. However, reserves take a longer view and incorporate expected losses over the instrument's life. The look-back period refers to the time period used to determine quantitative default risk estimates (normally 5-7 years under Basel II). As a qualitative calculation, loss reserves do not necessarily limit the analysis period.

There is no allowance made in loss reserves for unfunded commitments even though an expected loss is computed under Basel II for risk purposes. Loss reserves are more sensitive to incurred risks (such as obligor degradation), than expected loss (which is more forward-looking). Finally, charge-offs can differ significantly from economic loss because they do not include indirect and personnel costs associated with loss and recovery.

For this chapter, we focus on annualized expected loss rates for the purposes of pricing credit-linked instruments and obligations.

1.2 Loan Policy and Credit Risk

At the core of credit risk management is a well-crafted loan policy that addresses credit risk considerations, ratified by the bank's senior management or board. The loan policy, which is often called credit risk or credit policy, of a typical commercial bank incorporates the following:

- Mission and objectives, such as credit strategy, principles of lending practices, responsibility of relationship managers, the trade and business area, compliance requirements, loan and other credit products offered, and prohibited loans
- Lending guidelines such as the role of general and specialized loan committees and individual loan authorities for relationship managers, and procedures addressing exception management, collection efforts, and collateral
- Lending authority that identifies a bank's officers and establishes their responsibilities with regard to addressing the bank's lending limits, reporting of past due loans, and procedures for addressing non-accrual loans, charge-off policies, and external loan review
- Established operating procedures, such as credit evaluations, financial statements, collateral and debt service requirements, and loan administration, documentation, and disbursement

At a bank with more substantial trading exposure, the loan policy may more specifically and comprehensively address counterparty risk topics, such as the various approaches used to estimate potential exposures, netting, and collateral management.

The credit and loan policy is an essential component of bank corporate governance as it guides the bank in its core activity: to extend credit on a sound and collectable basis, while protecting the depositors and increasing the bank's value to the shareholders. While smaller banks may have one general loan policy, larger banks may complement the general loan policy with specific loan policies by product, market, or geographical level.

1.2.1 Mission and Objectives of the Credit Portfolio

In the loan policy, the overall composition, content, and size of the loan portfolio and the individual exposures within it constitute the mission and objectives of the credit portfolio.

The loan policy should determine the size and composition of the loan portfolio relative to the bank's balance sheet, and the bank's risk appetite relative to earnings, capital, and capabilities. The policy should consider the risk/reward trade-offs and establish guidelines for the bank to support its lending operations. An important consideration in determining the mission and objectives of the credit portfolio is the credit demand and the types of credit products offered by the bank.

The loan policy should also delineate the composition of the loan portfolio across the various types of credit products that are available: commercial, real estate, consumer, international, and government/sovereign. These limits reduce credit concentration risk. Additionally, the loan policy should establish limits for the minimum and maximum allowable loan amounts for each credit type. Banks further establish lending limits for industries and other exposures to diversify their loan portfolio. Finally, the policy should establish the in-house lending limit to borrowers in compliance with regulatory, legal, and other guidelines. (See Chapter 4 for a description of regulatory guidance on leveraged lending.)

The target market of the bank must also be defined as this helps the bank to serve its customers and supervise the individual loan exposures.

The loan policy may also state the types of loans it would not underwrite. Smaller banks may not be able to underwrite complex products or extend credit to certain types of businesses, due to local market, staffing, and other risk considerations. Many banks are reluctant to extend credit to certain businesses, for example, restaurants and bars, due to their historically high default rates.

For many banks securitization is an integral part of their business. This involves the creation and issuance of income generating securities, typically bonds, backed by the income generated by assets, loans, or other revenue sources. Securitization provides a number of benefits to both the banks and the investors in the securitized assets because securitization redistributes the inherent credit risks. Since securitization is a complex process, it should be supported by clear policy guidelines that address the products that can be securitized as well as the operational aspects of the securitization process.

Finally, as many banks engage in loan participation and syndicated lending, the bank's loan policy should also outline general standards for participating in syndicated lending.

1.2.2 Lending Guidelines

Financial performance standards, including acceptable sources of repayment and collateral requirements, provide a basis for the lending guidelines. Loan pricing standards may also be included in the lending guidelines to better link exposures to risks and pricing.

Financial performance standards outline key financial ratios, including debt service ratios, for the different types of credits the bank may offer. In addition, the bank may demand other criteria such as minimum sales volume, working capital, external credit ratings, and alternative access to financial markets. Moreover, the policy should also define the types of acceptable financial information sources, which the potential borrower must provide initially and on an on-going basis. Typically, with more complex and larger loans, the bank requires or expects more detailed information from the borrower.

In many cases, banks complement their internal evaluation with external credit references, including credit checks. The loan policy should outline how and when the bank should use additional external information from credit rating agencies or from credit bureaus.

The loan policy should list acceptable types of collateral and their respective loan-to-value limits. Similarly, "haircuts" on publicly traded securities should also be listed. The loan policy should state acceptable repayment periods for loans, including balloon payments.

By incorporating a bank's loan pricing principles into the loan policy, the governance structure of the bank can set acceptable levels of portfolio revenues, and may outline the various fees collected by the bank for the specific loan exposures. These principles and policies typically address computations of the bank's cost of funds and overhead costs, as well as the approaches to quantify acceptable risk-adjusted return.

How tightly these policies and guidelines are written reflects the bank's risk awareness. There is a large variation on the standards banks use, and as a result, bank supervisors take time to analyze the quality of these statements, and to evaluate the overall appropriateness of these standards in light of the bank's activities, performance, and risk levels.

1.2.3 Loan Authority

The credit policy should outline how credit is extended by the bank, and should identify those who are authorized to transact on behalf of the bank, as well as the size and limit of the transactions they may undertake.

Typically, loan officers have authorization to make and execute routine credit decisions, but the loan policy should outline how a loan authorization and approval is escalated for more complicated transactions. It is essential to have clearly defined procedures and established authority limits.

One of the ways loan authority can reduce credit risk is to have dual controls, as when the loan officer and the credit analyst must both agree that the loan should be extended.

The loan policy should also describe the highest authority within the bank that can make credit decisions on its behalf. Often, it is the bank's entire board but in many cases—due to the complexity of transactions, specialized understanding of the environment, timing and competitive pressures, or the need for flexibility—there are specialized board level loan committees that deal with complex loans, and act as the highest lending authority of the bank.

1.2.4 Operating Guidelines

Documentation and reporting standards, along with guidelines outlining the calculation of the allowance of loan losses, loan collections, and charge-offs, constitute the operating guidelines of the loan policy.

A solid loan policy should establish the various internal and legal documents the bank should gather in the underwriting process. Typically, internal documents include the "paper trail" of credit applications, credit and financial analysis, and credit memoranda, as well as the committee minutes documenting the loan decision. External documents can include appraisals, valuations, certificates of insurance or insurability, mortgages, and other legal documents that provide clear support, evidence, and documentation for the loan.

The flow of information to senior management and the board is essential to monitor the overall loan portfolio performance and, by extension, that of the bank. Typically, the policy states the types and frequency of reports to be produced on delinquent loans (non-accruing, non-performing, or charged off), portfolio composition and concentrations, and policy exceptions as well as the level of risk and potential losses.

Finally, the loan policy should outline procedures for dealing with delinquent borrowers and for determining and documenting collection attempts, and guidelines that specify charge-off requirements.

1.3 Credit Risk Assessment Framework

This section assumes prior exposure to basic credit analysis and focuses on a credit risk assessment framework that is used to value credit-linked obligations, such as loans, bonds, and lines of credit, as well as assessing the risk of those obligations.

The credit risk assessment framework has two parts. The first relates to the underwriting or originating process itself, that is, assessing the stand-alone credit worthiness of a borrower and pricing that credit risk accordingly. The second relates to the ongoing monitoring of credit, and any resulting adjustment to loan pricing.

1.3.1 Credit Risk Assessment in the Underwriting Process

The objective of the underwriting process is to make a lending decision. The underwriting process follows a number of critical steps, as outlined in Figure 1.3.

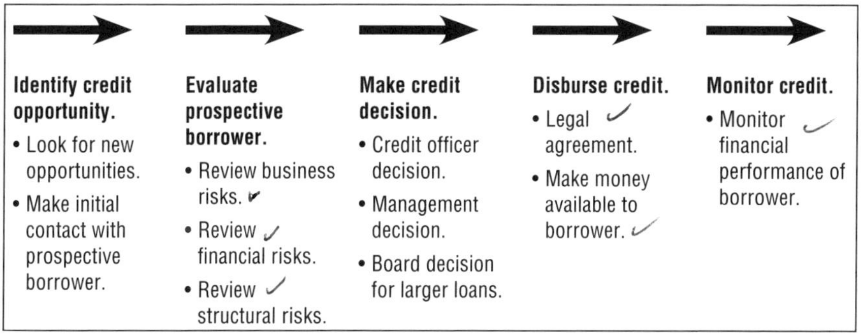

FIGURE 1.3 Steps in the Credit Process

This process is covered in detail in Chapter 4 of *Foundations of Financial Risk*, however a summary is provided here.

As discussed in Section 1.2, a bank's credit loan policy should form the bedrock of its underwriting process and direct bankers to identify new credit opportunities accordingly. Once a proposed credit product complies with credit risk policy, then the process of credit assessment or the evaluation of the prospective borrower (i.e., assessing risk as measured by the borrower's ability to repay) should begin. Credit assessment is not an exact science and no one factor, ratio, or other indicator alone determines if a particular loan or specific borrower is a suitable risk. The banking industry has developed numerous methods to help structure the credit process to enable detailed and thorough reviews of a prospective borrower's business, financial, and structural risks. These are discussed in greater detail below.

The output of the credit assessment process should be an objective and well-reasoned opinion of the overall risk associated with a particular loan or credit product. This risk needs to be calibrated in terms of appropriate loan pricing (see Section 1.3.2). The credit officer, management team, or board will make a credit decision in accordance with the bank's loan policy. Where the loan or credit is approved, credit is disbursed: a legal agreement is signed and money is made available to the borrower. Thereafter, the financial and operational performance of the borrower is monitored to ensure that its credit risk profile remains appropriate.

1.3.2 Credit Risk and Loan Pricing

One of the oldest sayings in banking is that "good pricing will never compensate for a bad credit decision." However, good pricing is the one way to compensate for credit decisions that may have been made by mistake. This is because it is the margin or spread that must absorb any predictable losses incurred in the portfolio and compensate for any unexpected losses that may subsequently arise.

The spread in each loan should be sufficient to compensate the bank for:

- The marginal cost of funds provided
- The overhead cost of maintaining the loan and the account
- The inherent risk of lending to this borrower while providing a return on the risk capital used to support the loan
- A sum to add to the bank's reserves

Many banks have created risk-adjusted, return-on-capital (RAROC) models to quantify the profitability of their lending activity and related capital requirements. However, loan pricing should not be the result of a simple formula, but rather of an informed negotiation. The bank should know what minimum spread—and profit—it should be willing to accept before entering into any agreement. The price of any loan is a direct cost to the borrower, whose focus is to minimize that cost. The outcome should be one that both sides consider fair and reasonable.

According to this relationship, the interest rate charged on the loan should equal the risk-free rate of interest and the markup [(PD × LGD) + S]. This provides compensation to the bank for the risk of default as well as the bank's spread:

$$\text{Loan interest rate} = \text{Risk-free rate} + \text{Compensation for expected losses} + \text{Spread}$$

$$\text{Loan interest rate} = \text{Risk-free rate} + (PD \times LGD) + S.$$

EXAMPLE

Bank B determines that Company B, a tire manufacturer, has a 2% chance of default on a one-year bullet loan of USD 1 million. The bank charges a 1.5% interest rate spread for firms in the tire industry, and the risk-free interest rate is 4%. Since there are no payments from Company B to Bank B during the year, default can only occur on the repayment date in one year. If Company B defaults, the bank expects to lose 60% of its promised payment.

In this case, PD = 2%, EAD = USD 1 million, LGD = 60%, D = 1 and S = 1.5%. The loss rate is 2% × 60%, or 1.2%, as there is a 2% chance of losing 60% of the loan principal. The total interest rate charged to Company B is 4% + 1.2% + 1.5% = 6.7%.

This simple example illustrates a general concept of loan pricing: the present value of the loan at initial funding or inception is USD 1 million, which is the discounted value of Company B's promised payment in one year (USD 1.067 million) at its discount rate or price (at inception) of 6.7%. This economic value of the loan may be different from the accounting value of the loan.

1.3.3 Revaluing the Loan

In banking, loan pricing can generally be adjusted, as allowed by agreement (for example, floating-rate loans tied to a specific index or the prime rate are typically repriced at full value at each reset date). However, in some cases repricing may be triggered due to an increase in the spread. This generally indicates that the credit risk of the borrower has risen and the lender should be compensated for this increased risk. In the same way, the bank may choose to revalue each loan consistent with the change in risk, as calculated using the company's PD. Another example of repricing stems from wholesale loan transactions, where loans are sold between banks at a price that reflects prevailing interest rates and credit ratings, and the transaction itself entails a markup.

Once the loan has been originated, the risks of the loan arise from revaluing, not repricing, the loan. Continuing with our example, the loan value after inception is:

Revalued loan (approximate) =
USD 1.067 million / {1 + [(New risk-free rate)
+ (New PD × New LGD) +New S]}

When PD × LGD is large, it is better to use the more accurate formula below:

Revalued loan =

USD 1.067 million × [1 – (New PD × New LGD)] /
[1 + (New risk-free rate + New S)]

In this formula, the numerator reflects expected loan repayments after considering default, and the denominator reflects the market cost of capital and the bank's cost of capital.

Loan revaluation affects the values at which the loan is recorded on the bank's balance sheet. Loans are recorded at their expected value (i.e., the increased expectation of default reduces the book value of the loan, which has to be adjusted by specific loan loss provisions in the loan loss reserve). Thus, the revaluation materially affects the financial position of the bank: it impacts both income and financial position.

Under either formula, changes to the initial parameters affect loan value.

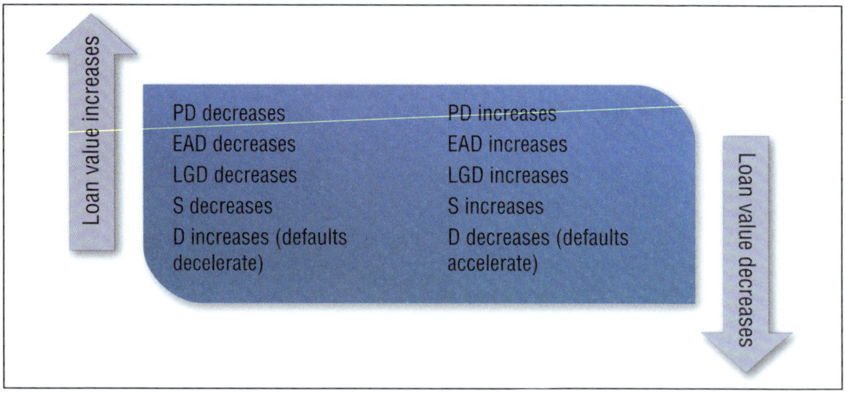

FIGURE 1.4 Changes in Loan Value

For example, Company B produces tires for global consumption: if the tire industry experiences adverse structural changes, Company B's PD and LGD may increase simultaneously, while D falls, causing the loan value to drop (this would be an example of spread risk). Alternatively, if Company

B experiences no changes, but bank credit tightens, S increases and thus reduces the current value of the loan.

EXAMPLE

Six months after Bank B provided the USD 1 million loan to Company B, a new competitor enters the tire industry. Company B decides to cut its prices in response to this competitive threat. However, the reduction in prices results in a write-down in the value of Company B's inventory. In this scenario, PD increases from 2% to 10%, and the LGD increases from 60% to 75%. If Bank B could reprice the loan, the new rate would be:

$$4\% + (10\% \times 75\%) + 1.5\% = 4\% + 7.5\% + 1.5\% = 13\%.$$

However, the bank is unable to change the interest payment on the loan, thus the value of the loan changes from:

$$\text{USD 1 million} / (1+ 0.067/2) = 1 \text{ million} / (1+0.0335) = 967{,}586$$

to:

$$\text{USD 1 million} / (1+ 0.13/2) = 1 \text{ million} / (1+ 0.065) = 938{,}967.$$

This is a decrease in value—a loss—of USD 28,619.

As the PD increase is substantial, the bank's auditors and regulators may require the bank management to make a specific loan loss provision for this particular loan, to reflect the decreased expected value of the loan. The revaluation of the loan decreased its value by USD 28,619. Thus, the bank would then reduce its earnings by the specific loan loss provision charge of USD 28,619 and increase the loan loss reserve by the same amount. The increase in the loan loss reserve reduces the book value of the loan from USD 1 million to USD 971,381.

1.4. Inputs to Credit Models

While the basic concepts of credit risk management (probability of default, exposure at default, recovery rate, etc.), are simple to understand, agreement about the concepts is not always translated into specific figures representing the credit risk of a loan portfolio. Indeed, even minor variations in assumptions can result in large differences in credit risk ratings. This may have far-reaching effects on a bank's ability to measure and effectively manage its credit risk, on its operations, and on its compliance with regulatory guidelines.

Beyond the issue of the accurate credit measurement is a more fundamental matter: the importance of understanding the information that drives the borrower's business. Here the challenge lies in the correct assessment of the credit exposure in terms of quantitative methodologies.

1.4.1 The Probability of Default (PD)

Banks calculate an obligor's PD based on many different models; this section describes some of the most common models. A bank might rely on a combination of causal models, historical frequency models, credit scoring models and credit rating agency models to assess a borrower's PD. All of these models may be adjusted based on behavioral factors, such as the potential for moral hazard and adverse selection (defined below).

Causal models

Causal models seek to identify the causes of default and assess the probability of the causes to determine the probability of default. For example, an individual risk model may suggest that an individual will default on a home loan only when the value of the home drops below the loan value, when the LTV ratio exceeds 100%, and the homeowner simultaneously becomes unemployed. If the probability of housing values falling to that level is judged to be 10%, and the probability of job loss is judged to be 15%, then the default probability can be estimated at 1.5%.[1]

Historical frequency models

Historical frequency models assign an obligor to an obligor class based on the risk characteristics of the borrower at the time the loan was originated, and estimate the default probability based on the historical default rate of the members of that particular class. Typical class choices for corporations may include the industry, the size of the corporation, or other variables. For example, if tire manufacturers have a historical default rate of 3% on their loans, a new loan applicant from the industry may also be judged to have a PD of 3%.

Credit scoring models

Credit scoring models resemble historical frequency models, but they include a wider class of comparables, with mathematical adjustments for the importance and weight of different characteristics. In many parts of the world, they are used to grade the obligations of SMEs for whom there

1 This assumes probabilistic independence of the two events. If the events are correlated–and the 2007–9 global financial crisis suggests that these two events exhibit a high degree of interdependence in certain areas–the default probability is higher.

is often a shortage of reliable financial information. For example, smaller firms may be three times more likely to default than larger firms in the same industry on average, while one industry may have a default rate that is half of the average for other industries. A credit scoring model would include statistical information for firms of all different industries and sizes to calibrate a default probability estimate for a particular company.

Credit scoring is frequently used in analyzing retail credits because retail borrowers are typically homogenous and numerous, and the information gathered on individual retail borrowers is considerably more standardized than the financial statements provided by corporate borrowers.

Credit scoring models are also used for corporate lending. Chapter 2 explains structural models used for determining PDs for corporate borrowers in more detail. The key component of these models is data on the borrower and this information may not be easily accessible or suffer from reliability or other quality problems. The Basel II Accord outlined the use of the Internal Ratings Based (IRB) approach to risk evaluation, which demands access to relevant loan information with at least a five-year history. Chapter 4 will discuss this and other regulatory approaches to quantifying credit risk and credit risk capital in more detail.

Scorecards

Another approach is the use of a "scorecard." This is less quantitative and more judgmental or qualitative. It is particularly useful when there is a limited amount of up-to-date and public information available about the borrower. These scorecard models are particularly useful for SMEs. The scorecard expands on the quantitative model by explicitly incorporating qualitative judgments about the borrower. Most scorecard models rate the riskiness of the borrower on a granular scale, where the continuum ranges from "low-risk borrower" to "borrower in default." Chapter 2 discusses SME credit evaluation and scorecards in greater detail.

Credit rating agency models

In markets where credit ratings are issued by credit rating agencies (CRAs) such as Moody's Investors Services (Moody's), Standard & Poor's (S&P), and Fitch Ratings (Fitch), banks may use these credit ratings as a guide to estimating PD. This is done by treating each credit rating as a homogeneous obligor class, and assigning PD to an individual obligor based on the rating. When calculating the PD of a business or an issue, the rating captures the PD on a one-year time horizon. At the same time, the rating also captures an expectation of recovery in the event of default.

For example, in March 2014, Standard and Poor's published five-year historical default rates for all companies, by starting credit rating.

From/to	AAA	AA	A	BBB	BB	B	CCC/C	D	NR
AAA	50.38	26.84	4.86	0.83	0.22	0.17	0.08	0.36	16.25
AA	1.58	49.88	24.97	3.87	0.62	0.42	0.05	0.37	18.24
A	0.09	5.41	53.77	15.27	2.25	0.81	0.18	0.65	21.56
BBB	0.03	0.56	10.31	49.37	7.80	2.58	0.43	2.26	26.66
BB	0.01	0.08	1.18	12.56	29.14	11.32	1.36	8.66	35.70
B	0.02	0.04	0.34	1.70	10.27	23.79	2.92	21.32	39.61
CCC/C	0.00	0.00	0.15	0.77	2.77	11.56	2.93	48.33	33.49

FIGURE 1.5 Five-year Global Corporate Average Transition Rates, 1981-2013 (%)
Source: Standard and Poor's Default, Transition, and Recovery: 2013 Annual Global Corporate Default Study and Rating Transitions, March 19, 2014

Transition rates compare average rating grades at the start of a particular time frame and at the end of the period. Figure 1.5 references five-year rates, however one-year, three-year, or seven-year rates are also available. It may be surprising to see that on average 3.64% of investment-grade rated (AAA-BBB) issuers defaulted in a five-year period, and that the rate was 2.26% for issuers initially rated BBB.

Nevertheless, it also demonstrates that higher ratings tend to be more stable than lower ratings. On average, 50.38% of issuers rated AAA at the outset were still rated AAA after five years compared with 23.79% of B rated issuers who were still rated B after 5 years at the end of the period.

Dynamic models

Dynamic PD models estimate the likely changes in default probability over time. In practice, dynamic models are constructed in many different ways, but one of the best-known dynamic PD models is based on the ratings migration model of Moody's. In this model, Moody's reports the historical annual migration rates of obligors from one credit rating class to another (from Aaa to D). These values are reported in a ratings migration matrix, shown in Figure 1.6.

From /To:	Aaa	Aa	A	Baa	Ba	B	Caa	Ca-C	WR	Default
Aaa	87.08%	8.33%	0.63%	0.00%	0.03%	0.00%	0.00%	0.00%	3.94%	0.00%
Aa	0.90%	84.50%	8.46%	0.51%	0.07%	0.02%	0.01%	0.00%	5.51%	0.02%
A	0.05%	2.43%	86.06%	5.56%	0.55%	0.11%	0.03%	0.00%	5.15%	0.06%
Baa	0.04%	0.17%	3.96%	85.18%	3.94%	0.73%	0.15%	0.02%	5.64%	0.17%
Ba	0.01%	0.05%	0.33%	5.60%	75.72%	7.31%	0.59%	0.06%	9.27%	1.06%
B	0.01%	0.03%	0.11%	0.30%	4.50%	73.52%	5.94%	0.57%	11.32%	3.71%
Caa	0.00%	0.02%	0.02%	0.11%	0.37%	8.58%	62.58%	3.58%	11.94%	12.81%
Ca-C	0.00%	0.00%	0.06%	0.00%	0.37%	2.03%	9.10%	36.42%	14.03%	38.00%

FIGURE 1.6 Average One-Year Letter Rating Migration Rates, 1970–2013 (Moody's)
Source: Moody's Special Comment: Annual Default Study: Corporate Default and Recovery Rates, 1920-2013, February 28, 2014

This matrix shows the historical likelihood that a Baa-rated obligor would stay at a Baa rating or higher over a one-year period. Based on these data, a Baa-rated obligor has an 85.18% chance of remaining Baa in one year, with about a 3.96% chance of upgrading to an A rating, a 4.67% chance of downgrading to a Ba or B rating, and a 5.64% chance of having the rating withdrawn.

Assuming the independence of rating migration from year to year, this table can be used to compute probabilities of default over multiple years as well as for a single year, as in the example shown below.

From/ To:	Aaa	Aa	A	Baa	Ba	B	Caa	Ca-C	WR	Default
Aaa	51.31%	23.59%	5.23%	0.37%	0.33%	0.04%	0.04%	0.00%	19.01%	0.09%
Aa	2.73%	44.85%	21.27%	4.09%	0.75%	0.27%	0.09%	0.01%	25.59%	0.34%
A	0.19%	7.41%	49.89%	14.49%	2.62%	0.85%	0.19%	0.01%	23.60%	0.75%
Baa	0.18%	1.01%	11.74%	47.38%	8.44%	2.72%	0.54%	0.07%	26.32%	1.62%
Ba	0.04%	0.16%	1.99%	11.81%	26.54%	10.93%	1.45%	0.11%	39.00%	7.98%
B	0.03%	0.04%	0.25%	1.63%	6.38%	21.90%	5.29%	0.61%	44.76%	19.10%
Caa	0.00%	0.00%	0.02%	0.54%	1.52%	7.63%	9.64%	1.02%	42.06%	37.58%
Ca-C	0.00%	0.00%	0.00%	0.00%	0.00%	3.12%	1.70%	4.37%	38.49%	52.32%

* Last cohort formed on 1/1/2009

FIGURE 1.7 Average Five-Year Letter Rating Migration Rates, 1970–2013 (Moody's)
Source: Moody's Special Comment: Annual Default Study: Corporate Default and Recovery Rates, 1920-2013, February 28, 2014

Internal Ratings Approach

Some banks use their own estimates of PD, calculated using statistics from CRAs such as Moody's or S&P and specific criteria such as a minimum floor. Figure 1.8 demonstrates an internal rating scale and corresponding PDs based on the one-year, issuer-weighted global default rates published by Moody's, with a 3 bp (basis point) floor.

Internal Rating	Probability of Default
iaaa	0.03%
iaa	0.05%
iA+	0.07%
ia	0.08%
iA-	0.09%
iBBB+	0.16%
iBBB	0.17%
iBBB-	0.26%
iBB+	0.67%
iBB	0.75%
iBB-	1.73%
iB+	2.32%
iB	3.54%
iB-	5.98%
iCCC	54.13%
iD	100.00%

FIGURE 1.8 An Example of a Typical Bank's Internal Rating Scale

Moral hazard

In bank lending, moral hazard refers to the tendency of an obligor to change its behavior after a loan has been originated. Without moral hazard, we could assume that high-risk obligors would be more reluctant to borrow because of the high interest rates they would be charged. Moral hazard explains why such an obligor may not care about the interest rate being charged, that is, if it has no intention to repay the loan fully.

Alternatively, the obligor may use the loan proceeds for purposes not sanctioned by the lender and these uses may actually increase the risk of default. Alternatively, the borrower may use an existent credit line recklessly thereby increasing the PD. For these reasons, banks must estimate PDs based on assumptions about the applicability of moral hazard to particular lending situations. They may decide not to extend credit where moral hazard is judged likely to be a problem.

Adverse selection

Adverse selection is frequently confused with moral hazard, but it is different. In a banking context, adverse selection occurs when a customer chooses a loan product or feature that benefits the customer, but affects the bank adversely for reasons not necessarily known at the time of origination. For example, a customer may choose a mortgage with payments that are low at first but then increase over time because the customer knows it will have trouble making higher payments in the later years of the loan. If the bank makes this type of mortgage with the same default assumptions used for ordinary mortgages, it will underestimate the risk of default.

Sometimes adverse selection is not caused by the customer, but by other circumstances. For example, some high-risk customers may not be able to qualify for fixed-rate loans. Banks have been known to offer innovative products that reflect the limited payment capacity of these borrowers. Recognizing that these customers sometimes are able to take variable-rate loans that offer initially lower interest rates, called "teasers," banks have offered such loans to low-quality borrowers. Since these loans are underwritten for lower credit-quality borrowers, and it is reasonable to expect that a higher proportion of low credit-quality borrowers would be interested in these loans, the bank's credit risk models should consider these circumstances explicitly. Thus, banks should use a higher average default rate for such "teaser" variable rate loans.

1.4.2 The Exposure at Default (EAD)

In some cases, the bank's exposure at the point of default is obvious (in a loan, it is simply the value of the remaining loan payments). In other cases, the exposure is not at all obvious, as the following examples illustrate.

Line of credit

An undrawn line of credit may appear at first to have little exposure in the event of default. However, it is precisely in times of financial difficulty that a company is likely to draw down its line of credit. Hence, the exposure of an undrawn credit line is generally considered to be similar to that of a loan.

Counterintuitively, borrowers with higher credit ratings who have access to undrawn, or unused, lines of credit pose a greater challenge than poorly rated borrowers. With limited resources, banks tend to focus their attention on the marginal loans and typically monitor lower-rated borrowers more closely than their best customers. Thus, a bank monitoring its higher-rated borrowers should also identify those lines where the higher-rated borrower inexplicably starts to draw down on the line.

Collateral

When a bank requires the borrower to post collateral, it is trying to protect itself against the risk that the borrower or obligor does not pay on time or at all. In this case, the value of the collateral is deducted from the value of the gross exposure to determine the bank's Exposure at Default (EAD) and Loss Given Default (LGD). This is a simple matter if the value of the collateral is known (such as high-quality corporate bonds or US government bonds), but it becomes more difficult if the collateral value is uncertain (such as real estate). For example, a mortgage loan is secured by property, and property values fluctuate. A repo (see Chapter 3) is secured by market-traded instruments, and hence its LGD may change continuously. If the collateral exceeds the loan balance, and recovery can be considered to be almost certain at default, the LGD could be determined to be zero.

Variable exposure

Some contracts, such as swaps or variable rate loans, require an obligor to pay an uncertain amount to the bank in the future. In these cases, banks use market risk models to estimate the exposure to an obligor in the event of default.

Ability to Net

In some situations, exposure to an obligor may be offset by the bank's obligations to the same obligor, assuming that there is a legal right to offset exposures. For example, if an obligor has taken out a loan from the bank but simultaneously entered an FX forward trade with the bank, in the event of default, the bank may be able to terminate the FX trade and net the gains on the trade against the losses on the loan. The ability to net depends on the legal environment as well as the specific contracts agreed between the bank and the obligor.

Banks may require their borrowers to maintain a certain deposit volume at the bank, some of which is kept in a low-interest bearing account that the borrower may not access freely or at all. These deposits are called compensating balances and provide multiple benefits for the bank. First, compensating balances allow the bank to net some of the exposure it may have in case of default by taking funds from this specific deposit account once the borrower defaults. Second, because these compensating balances cannot be withdrawn on short notice, if at all, they are not considered transaction accounts and are able to provide a stable source of funding to the bank, reducing its reliance on more volatile external interbank-based funding sources. Third, since the compensating balances reduce the net amount lent to the borrower, the earned return on the loan is increased.

For many banks, Exposure at Default is an integral part of counterparty credit risk assessment. One example of the EAD calculation for each counterparty could be 95% potential exposure less recovery. The default loss distribution would be based on the probability of default for each individual counterparty being measured at a 99.5% confidence level.

However, the challenge is the estimate of the potential exposure at default, which is not simple. Some of the factors that are typically considered when computing exposures include:

- Returns, volatilities, and correlations of individual instruments, market factors, and risk factors
- The aging of trades and the effects of possible revaluation of trades and positions caused by changing market circumstances
- Possible offsets between long and short positions with the same counterparty and/or instrument
- Availability of netting and the impact of or access to margin
- Specific valuation considerations, including cash flow patterns, possible path dependencies, and the existence of optionalities
- Portfolio considerations, product concentrations, and legal considerations with respect to the counterparty

Chapter 2 describes counterparty risk in more detail.

1.4.3 The Loss Given Default (LGD)

Several factors influence the expected loss rate of a bank given the default of the obligor. Typically, the most important drivers of LGD are:

- Debt type and seniority
- Macroeconomic environment
- Industry
- Firm-specific capital structure

In general, the more senior the debt is, the lower the loss given default. However, the LGD depends on the quality of the underlying assets and the existence of collateral or secondary repayment support. Macroeconomic factors affect the value of collateral, and therefore affect recovery in default. Industry factors also affect collateral value. "Firm-specific capital structure" refers to the ability of a lender to access the general funds of a corporation to satisfy the debt. For example, a holder of a senior note may have first access to the collateral, but depending on the amount and types of other debt issued by the company, may not have the ability to make a claim against general funds in bankruptcy.

There are also numerous special considerations for LGD determination such as recourse, the ability to assign the loan, obligor asset type, and payment delays.

Ultimately it is the bank's external environment which impacts the LGD through the RR. The RR is lower when default rates are higher because of lower demand for defaulted assets, as there may be an excess supply of assets and collateral that is likely to depress prices: typically, RR is considerably lower during economic downturns. That is why many banks faced with accelerating defaults during challenging economic cycles often turn to splitting off the non-performing assets in a separate asset management unit—sometimes referred to as a bad bank—with the task of ensuring that assets are sold off as the economy improves.

Additionally, in the case of banks with large trading operations, counterparty defaults may be triggered because the value of the counterparty assets starts to decline or the assets fail to generate adequate profits.

Recourse

If an obligation is "full recourse" to the obligor, the bank has the ability to place a claim against all of the assets of the obligor in order to satisfy its obligations. In a full recourse loan, if the collateral is insufficient to satisfy the debt in the event of default, the bank will attempt to recover additional funds from the obligor.

In a "non-recourse loan," the lender can only use the loan's collateral for repayment in the event of default. When the lender does not require additional payment guarantees, it assumes a greater lending risk. As a result, such non-recourse lending is normally extended only to the bank's best clients.

Relative to non-recourse loans, full recourse loans generally reduce LGD, since there is some chance of additional recovery, whereas non-recourse loan recovery is limited to the value of the collateral. If the non-recourse loan is made without additional secondary repayment support, the bank's exposure will depend on the otherwise unencumbered assets that the borrower has beyond the claim of other lenders and creditors.

Both in international lending and in counterparty credit risk assessment, it is essential to recognize that jurisdictional differences between countries exist when it comes to recourse. Some jurisdictions are more creditor-friendly and offer creditors greater, faster, and legally binding access to secure payment on their claims. In other parts of the world, the debtor may have broader legal opportunities to delay repayment and even cancel out the debt.

Assignment

Loans may be assignable in the event of default. For example, if a subsidiary of a company defaults on its obligation, the bank may have insisted on a guarantee or an assignment clause that requires the parent company to assume responsibility for the loan in the event of default. In this case, the bank substitutes the expected LGD of the assignee for the LGD of the obligor.

In case of assignment, it is important to understand the legal relationships between the companies involved in the assignment (in particular their legal capacity to act as a party to the assignment). This consideration is particularly important when the legal domiciles of the subsidiary and the parent company are different, and the contract must satisfy legal and other rules in different jurisdictions.

Obligor asset type

If the obligor owns assets that are readily saleable to satisfy its obligations in default, such as receivables or high-quality products, its LGD assessment will be lower than that of a company without saleable assets. For example, if a bank enters into identical transactions with a trading company and an electricity generating company, it would consider the electricity generating company to have a lower LGD than the trading company, based on the assumption that it was a regulated entity and had assets that are available to help satisfy its obligations in default. The electricity generating company may have significant investments in plant, equipment, distribution networks, and contracts that are valuable due to their contribution to everyday life. By contrast, when trading companies default, they have fewer tangible assets (except for their inventory and receivables) for use as security against their obligations.

Delays

In some cases, a loan or a bond may eventually be repaid after default, such as when sovereign bonds resume payments after a rescheduling. This can also arise in situations where a company's ability to pay has been compromised by the nonpayment of a major receivable. In these cases, the present value of the obligation can be thought of as a partial recovery in the event of default. The loss rate or LGD is therefore the percentage of present value lost to repayment deferral.

Recovery rates, which impact LGD and by extension EL, vary according to security position, stage in the economic cycle, and types of industry. The following table compiled by Moody's lists the corporate recovery rates according to security position.

	Issuer-weighted			Volume-weighted		
Lien Position	**2013**	**2012**	**1982-2013**	**2013**	**2012**	**1982-2013**
1st Lien Bank Loan	75.1%	66.4%	66.3%	67.7%	66.8%	60.2%
2nd Lien Bank Loan*	78.7%	17.4%	32.1%	69.2%	15.3%	27.5%
Sr. Unsecured Bank Loan	n.a.	n.a.	47.1%	n.a.	n.a.	40.2%
Sr. Secured Bond	57.7%	51.2%	52.2%	58.8%	28.4%	47.7%
Sr. Unsecured Bond	43.8%	43.0%	37.2%	29.2%	40.1%	37.8%
Sr. Subordinated Bond*	20.7%	33.7%	31.0%	26.6%	39.3%	25.9%
Subordinated Bond	26.4%	37.3%	31.4%	33.7%	32.1%	25.5%
Jr. Subordinated Bond	n.a.	n.a.	24.7%	n.a.	n.a.	17.1%

*The average recovery for 2012 and for 2013 second-lien bank loans were based on three observations. The average recovery for 2013's senior subordinated bonds was based on four issuers.

FIGURE 1.9 Average Corporate Debt Recovery Rates Measured by Trading Prices

Source: Moody's Special Comment: Annual Default Study: Corporate Default and Recovery Rates, 1920-2013, February 28, 2014

Internal Rating Approach

Many banks devise their own internal rating approach to estimate recovery rates on various types of borrowers, exposures, and counterparties. Such rating approaches incorporate external, counterparty, and facility-specific considerations, including the complexity of the deal. Based on these considerations, a continuum of rating grades is created which delivers an expected RR and assigned LGD.

	Expected Recovery Rate		
Internal Rating	>	<=	Assigned LGD
i1	85%	100%	10%
i2	75%	85%	20%
i3	65%	75%	30%
i4	55%	65%	40%
i5	45%	55%	50%
i6	35%	45%	60%
i7	25%	35%	70%
i8	15%	25%	80%
i9	5%	15%	90%
i10	0%	5%	100%
iDefault	0%	0%	100%

FIGURE 1.10 Example of a Bank's Internal Rating Approach, Expected RR, and Assigned LGD

1.4.4 Duration (D)

Duration to default refers to the expected timeframe in which default is expected to occur. For example, if a new three-year loan has a 2% probability of defaulting in the first year, a 4% probability of defaulting in the second year, and a 7% probability of default in the third year, the expected duration of the default time is the weighted average, or

$$[(0.02 \times 1) + (0.04 \times 2) + (0.07 \times 3)]/[0.13] = 2.4 \text{ years}.$$

Of all the risk factors in loan pricing, the duration to default is likely the least significant. The timing of default is influenced by numerous factors, but it has importance because of its linkage to EAD and by extension to EL. For example, many loans amortize their principal over time, so an increase in time to default is associated with a reduction in exposure at the time of the default, as the value of the principal has dropped.

Some instruments are affected by obligor "seasoning": the tendency of obligors not to default in the initial stages of a contract. For example, if a healthy firm receives a bank loan, it is unlikely that conditions will deteriorate overnight and cause immediate default, but after a few years pass, the firm may not have been able to maintain its strong position. Recognizing this, the bank may reduce PD estimates in the first few years and increase them in later years to reflect the impact of loan seasoning. Loan seasoning also reflects the impact that longer-term economic cycles may have on the frequency of default.

Lending is pro-cyclical, increasing during periods of expansion, when credit is widely available and default rates are typically low. However, as the economy contracts, lending volume dries up, partly because borrowers are less comfortable taking on new debt and partly because lenders are becoming increasingly concerned with repayment. Economic contraction squeezes marginal borrowers, further increasing the financial and business stress on these entities, which in turn increases the likelihood of default. The duration to default should reasonably consider potential cyclical changes as well.

1.4.5 The Spread (S)

The loan spread is a function of a bank's direct costs of originating and managing loans and its required rate of return on capital. In turn, the cost of capital is influenced by the returns the bank earns on its other investments (i.e., its opportunity cost of capital) and other business activities. Thus, the funding cost of capital is affected by forces internal to the bank and by external capital market forces. For example, as a bank's available capital shrinks, its loan spread will widen to generate sufficiently high returns. Also, as market spreads widen, the bank's loan spreads will follow suit, because as its funding cost increases, the bank seeks to pass on these added expenses to the borrower, either through pricing power or floating rate loans.

S is the most subjective element of the loan pricing formula and can also be used to control the bank's exposure to loans. Increases in S will reduce the bank's competitiveness in the loan market and reduce its market share, whereas decreases in S will have the opposite effect. Therefore a bank looking to reduce its capital allocation to loans can do so by managing its loan spreads. Increasing loan spreads will depress the demand for the bank's loans and reduce origination activity, causing a natural reduction in capital allocation to loans.

A bank can reduce its spread not only by reducing the mark-up on the cost of funds that it charges to its borrowers, but also—as was seen in the run up to the global financial crisis—by reducing stringent underwriting standards through diluting risk grades, and not appropriately adjusting the spreads. By lowering the spread on lower credit quality borrowers, the bank can aggressively court new business and grow rapidly, but at the expense of increased probability of default, higher losses in case of default, and unexpected losses.

1.4.6 Special Considerations for Guaranteed Debt

When an obligation is subject to a guarantee, the obligor's financial responsibility is assumed by the guarantor in the event of default. Examples of this include parent guarantees (issued by the parent company of a subsidiary), letters of credit (issued by banks), and surety bonds (issued by insurance companies). In the presence of a guarantee, the bank first needs to evaluate the legal strength of the guarantee. If the contract is sound, then the bank may substitute the credit attributes of the guarantor for the credit attributes of the obligor in its decision to award credit. In other words, the credit evaluation is extended to include the creditworthiness (including both the ability and willingness to honor such a commitment) of the guarantor.

Generally, it will be the case that a guarantee will reduce PD, but its effect on LGD will be determined according to the specifics of a given situation. For example, a parent company may have much greater financial strength than its subsidiary, but if all its assets are encumbered, its LGD may be higher than that of the subsidiary.

In some cases, the guarantor will hold less credit standing than the obligor at inception. For example, debt of a privately held corporation may be guaranteed personally by its owner. Though the owner may have little in the way of assets outside the corporation, the bank uses a guarantee of this type to reduce its LGD by being able to make a claim on the owner's assets in the event of default.

It should be noted here that under Basel II, in the calculation of LGD and EL, a zero value must be used for personal guarantees, even when the banker may be totally certain that the guarantor will be good for the amount of the guarantee if called upon. Furthermore, the Basel Committee expects banks to claim against pledged assets first and recover as much as possible from them before the bank turns to the guarantor to make good any shortfall. In reality, banks will usually call in a guarantee first before foreclosing on any collateral assets.

1.5 Summary

This chapter describes a common credit risk assessment framework that is applied to retail, corporate, and sovereign credit repricing risk.

Distinguishing credit risk from market risk

- Credit risk is more important than market risk for many banks
- Credit risk is a form of performance risk that is associated with the non-performance of a financial contract, or financial aspects of non-performance in any contract
- Many credit risk drivers relate to market risk drivers, such as the impact of market conditions on default probabilities
- PD is the probability of default: the risk that the obligor, or borrower, will fail to make full and timely repayment of its financial obligations over a given time horizon (duration); also called EDF (Expected Default Frequency)
- LGD is the loss given default: the percentage of the exposure realized as a loss if there is a default
- EAD is the exposure at default: the expected exposure at the time of default
- EL is the expected loss: the average expected credit loss over a given time period
- UL is the unexpected loss: the maximum loss at a degree of statistical confidence in excess of expected loss
- RR is the recovery rate: the proportion of the EAD the bank recovers in default.
- D is the duration to default
- S is the spread for pricing credit-linked obligations

Loan policy and credit risk

A well-crafted loan policy addresses credit risk considerations and incorporates:

- Mission and objectives, such as credit strategy, principles of lending practices, and lending guidelines such as underwriting process, standards, and collateral
- Lending authorities such as the responsibilities of the bank's officers related to the bank's legal lending limit and house lending limits
- Reporting of past due loans, procedures addressing non-accrual loans, charge off policy, external loan review

- Established operating procedures, such as credit evaluations, financial statements, collateral and debt service requirements, and loan administration, documentation, and disbursement

Credit risk assessment framework

- The objective of the underwriting process is to make a lending decision.
- A sound credit process follows a number of critical steps: i) identify a credit opportunity, ii) evaluate prospective borrower, iii) make credit decision, iv) disburse credit, v) monitor credit.
- The output of the credit assessment process should be an objective and well-reasoned opinion of the overall risk associated with a particular loan or credit product.
- This risk needs to be calibrated in terms of appropriate loan pricing.
- The rate of interest a bank charges on a loan can be approximated by the formula, rate = risk-free rate + (PD × LGD) + S, where (PD × LGD) + S represents the compensation required by the bank to accommodate the credit risk of the loan.
- Bank risk to credit exposure can be summarized by understanding how the repricing of debt obligations is influenced by these factors.

Input to credit models

- PD is the default probability, which can be estimated using historical default frequency, credit scoring, credit rating, moral hazard, and adverse selection considerations.
- Dynamic PD models have been built by Moody's and others to see how PDs change over time.
- EAD is the exposure at default: the maximum amount a bank could be exposed to on a customer obligation. It is sometimes fixed and sometimes variable.
- LGD is the loss given default, the estimated percentage of EAD lost in a default situation.
- LGD is influenced by collateral, by the variable liabilities of a company, and by the ability to net credit exposures with a company in default.
- LGD is influenced by debt type, asset type, recourse, assignment terms, and payment delays.
- D is the expected duration to default: the expected time until default, conditional on default occurring.
- S is a bank-determined or market-driven premium for credit risk of a particular type.

CHAPTER 2

The Risks of Credit Products

This chapter focuses on the risk drivers of the main classes of credit obligations for various obligor types that commonly constitute the portfolio of typical banks. Using examples, the chapter discusses five different types of obligors and their risk drivers. The focus is not facility-driven risk analysis: i.e., the discussion does not focus on the specific risks of individual credit products. Rather, it discusses the risk drivers of the different types of borrowers by identifying those factors that can impact the riskiness of a specific obligor, and by extension, the risk driver of the assets included in a bank's trading and banking books.

On completion of this chapter the reader will have an improved understanding of:

- The factors that impact the riskiness of different types of borrowers: retail customers, SMEs, corporates, counterparties, and sovereigns.
- How to link credit risk to retail economic factors. Understanding the key inputs in credit scoring models for retail borrowers.
- Assessing the credit risk of SME obligors; the usefulness of scorecards.
- Determining corporate credit risk by using structural models such as Altman's *Z*-score, Merton's distance-to-default, reduced form models such as Jarrow's and Turnbull's or by using ratings from credit rating agencies such as Moody's, Fitch Ratings, or Standard & Poor's.

- How counterparty credit differs from corporate credit: exposures may be netted; EAD may be variable; exposure is two-way.
- The importance of sovereign credit to bank asset and liquidity management. The key risk factors in sovereign credit arise from political risk, institutional risk, financial and economic risks, and susceptibility to event risk such as war or natural disaster.

2.1 Retail Credit Risks

Given the credit risk factors (PD, EAD, LGD, D, and S; see Chapter 1) for individual borrowers, banks can determine the risk and the associated pricing of retail credit products. Retail credit products include secured loans, such as residential mortgages and car loans, and unsecured loans, such as educational loans, credit card debt, and lines of credit (overdraft facilities).

The purpose of this section is to link credit risk factors to retail economic factors, in order to determine banks' repricing risks on retail lending products. The examples and tables that follow in this section focus on the US because of the availability of data, while recognizing that these examples will be directly and immediately applicable for some countries but less applicable for others. However, the principles of retail lending are universal: the performance of these individual products largely reflects overall economic performance, salary and income levels, wealth accumulation, and the relationship between consumption and saving both on the individual level and on the aggregate, economic level. Moreover, as retail credit products are largely homogenous, many banks consider these products as a commodity from a risk and strategy perspective.

2.1.1 Size of the Retail Credit Market in the US

As of December 2014, consumer credit outstanding (not including loans for real estate) in the US amounted to over USD 3.3 trillion. According to statistics issued by the Federal Reserve (the US central bank), financial institutions reported the following aggregates.

	Revolving	Non-revolving	Total
Commercial Banks	730.4	609.6	1,340.0
Pools of securitized assets	28.9	20.6	49.5
Other providers	128.5	1,793.8	1,922.3
Total	887.9	2,423.9	3,311.8

FIGURE 2.1 Consumer Credit by Major Providers, USD Billions, as of December 2014 (not seasonally adjusted)
Source: The Board of Governors of the Federal Reserve System (G19 release, Consumer Credit, updated monthly), as of December 2014, released January 2015.

These figures do not include any indebtedness secured by real estate (such as mortgages). Revolving loans have variable balances, and may be secured or unsecured (credit cards and lines of credit are examples of revolving loans). Non-revolving loans include automobile loans and all other loans not included in revolving credit (such as loans for mobile homes, education, boats, trailers, or general consumption); these loans may also be secured or unsecured.

Two figures in this table that warrant special mention are the USD 49.5 billion aggregate for pools of securitization and USD 1.9 trillion of "other providers". Pools of consumer-securitized assets peaked in the US at over USD 1.1 trillion in June 2008. The USD 49.5 billion reported in December 2014 is therefore a drop of 96%. This decline can be seen as a two pronged response to the global financial crisis: first, a precipitous drop in demand for securitized consumer debt and second, far-reaching changes in the regulation of the securitization market. Aside from real estate, the largest component of securitized debt is credit card debt.

The "other providers" category reflects positions held by non-banks, such as finance companies, credit unions, savings and loans (thrifts), the federal government, and non-financial businesses. The largest provider in this category is the US Federal government as a provider of student loans, which were USD 841.9 billion. Student debt has more than tripled in the US in the last ten years as the number of students going to university has increased. More of those students are borrowing to pay for their education and, due to increasing tuitions, the amounts borrowed have risen year-on-year. A high level of student debt and/or delinquency on student debt is likely to negatively impact borrowers' ability to secure future debt such as mortgages.

Revolving home equity loans	458.1
Other residential loans	1,576.3
Credit card & other revolving plans	636.7
Other consumer loans	578.7
Total (all assets)	15,047.0

FIGURE 2.2 Aggregate US Bank Balance Sheet (Selected Entries) December 2014 in USD Billions
Source: The Board of Governors of the Federal Reserve, H8 Release, February 13, 2015

From the first table, we can see that banks hold about 42% of the $3.3 trillion US consumer credit obligations outside of borrowing secured by real estate, of which less than 4% was securitized. Although the direct exposure banks have to the health of the retail credit sector has decreased in recent years as the non-banking financial sector has increased, it remains significant.

Combining the consumer credit figures for commercial banks in the first table with the banks' own figures for real estate related consumer credit shows that as a fraction of their assets, banks hold approximately 22% in retail obligations, of which 63% are related to real estate and 37% are non-real estate. When the real estate sector is robust, banks worry less about retail credit, but as the real estate sector weakens, consumer credit risk grows substantially. In countries such as the US where direct home ownership is high and financed through mortgages, the real estate sector is a significant risk factor determining the health of the financial system. According to research by McKinsey Global Institute, mortgages account for 74% of household debt in advanced economies and 43% of household debt in developing countries, where household loans also include borrowing for small businesses.

2.1.2 Consumer Credit Scoring in the US

At the retail level, the most important determinants of loan origination and pricing are the loan application and the individual credit score. In the US, credit scores are provided by credit scoring agencies, primarily by Equifax, Experian, and TransUnion. Individuals with better credit profiles and higher credit scores are able to secure more credit at lower interest rates.

The credit application generally includes information about the borrower's income, employment, assets, and liabilities. Assets typically include both financial and non-financial assets; the application may require a list of any security interests such as mortgages attached to such assets, particularly as these assets may serve as security or collateral for other loans. Real estate, financial securities, and other valuables are typically listed. Liabilities include both previously incurred loans and ongoing commitments to pay judgments, liens, and similar impairments to the assets.

In evaluating credits, many lenders turn to various credit scoring agencies in order to provide a comprehensive view of a borrower's credit score. A number of providers have developed credit scoring methodologies for use by credit scoring agencies. Fair Isaac Corporation (FICO) develops scoring models for Equifax and TransUnion, while Scorex, develops models for Experian. FICO reports that 90 of the largest 100 financial institutions in the US use FICO scores in their consumer lending decisions.

Generally speaking, the credit score includes 100 predictive factors, but the exact inputs and formulation of the score are kept confidential and differ among the credit scoring agencies. Inputs are drawn from information on an individual's credit record or new credit application, and from other sources. These predictive models are constantly being improved. It is important to note that in the US, the score may not consider an individual's race, sex, marital status, national origin, and religion. Other countries may have different rules regarding allowable inputs.

Although credit scores are far from being standardized, typical scores range between 300 and 850. Because the scores are calculated using slightly different algorithms, sometimes there are differences between the credit scores of a borrower. However, large differences are typically unusual. Instead, such differences reflect different sources of data used by the scoring agencies, different factor weights, and the agency's speed of updating information.

Some larger banks have developed their own credit scoring and credit utilization predictive models, based on their own credit experiences and the methodologies developed by credit scoring agencies. All these models assess credit risk based primarily on credit history and utilization, and not on current assets or income.

2.1.3 Credit Score Factors

According to FICO, payment history accounts for approximately 35% of its credit score. Payment history reflects the various accounts held by individuals, including credit cards, mortgage loans, and retail accounts. Patterns of late payments on existing debt have a significant negative effect on the rating, as do foreclosures, lawsuits, and other collection-related items.

Indebtedness accounts for about 30% of FICO's credit score. This includes actual debt balances and also debt capacity (i.e., the amount of potential indebtedness) although it is the total amount of debt used that the credit score reflects, and not the total amount of credit. Interestingly, the credit score is negatively impacted by not having any ongoing credit usage, i.e., not using available credit is considered as a negative factor by the agencies. Similarly, having credit levels very close to the total debt ceiling negatively impacts the overall credit score.

Approximately 10% of the overall score falls under a category that FICO categorizes as new credit, i.e., a penalty for those actively seeking new credit, or where annual credit monitoring may require ongoing credit checks. As a consequence, shopping around for credit—as many retail consumers do—may negatively impact an individual's credit score.

Another 15% percent of the FICO credit score measures the length of credit history; the longer the credit history, and the longer the average age of credits, the higher the credit rating.

Finally, approximately 10% of the FICO credit score considers the type of credit obligations an applicant may already have in place. For example, a good history of mortgage repayment has the most positive impact on the credit score.

A score above 680 is generally considered to be "prime," or high quality with low risk of default, while individuals with scores between 575 and 680 are generally classified as "subprime." Individuals with scores below 540 will generally be denied credit (a bankruptcy in the prior 7-10 years would cause a 160-220 point deduction on the credit score, and a delinquent account would subtract 70-120 points from the score). Even among borrowers with a prime score there is an internal gradation between good, very good, and excellent, which can significantly impact borrowing terms.

The factors in the description above vary around the world and also region by region.

2.1.4 Retail Credit Without Credit Scores

In the absence of credit scores, retail credit can be evaluated through credit references and other credit checks. This requires a precise listing of the potential borrower's income and expenses in addition to an extensive record of assets and liabilities. The bank then verifies these assets and liabilities and ensures that the assets are unencumbered and the liabilities are in good standing.

Using various yardsticks, banks evaluate the fixed expenses of the borrower to assess the ability to assume the new debt, factoring in personal conditions, such as family size and lifestyle choices. Typically, new debt should not exceed certain prudent and indicative income-to-debt-service measures, such as not more than 40% of income being used to service debt, and only 20% of income being used to pay real estate debt. These benchmarks are indicative: many banks take into consideration the wealth and social position of the borrower that may allow for borrowing in excess of prudent indicative guidelines.

In addition, the bank seeks to evaluate whether the borrower may have any contingent liabilities that can impair the ability to repay. Such contingent liabilities could stem from loans that small businesses assume through their owners, but in general, a large proportion of contingent liabilities stems from loan guarantees that individuals provide for friends and family. These loan guarantees can be triggered if the original borrower defaults, making the guarantor directly liable to repay the loan.

In countries where credit scoring is not legally or structurally practical, many banks have created credit registries or credit consortia that offer a listing of all debts, from small loans to large mortgages, that an individual borrower may have. These credit registries can also list guarantees and provide additional transparency for a bank making credit decisions.

2.1.5 Summary of Retail Credit Risk Drivers

At the individual obligor level, the major drivers of credit risk are the individual's assets, liabilities, income, impairments, payment history, recent credit application behavior, length of credit history, and type of credit obligations held. From a bank's perspective, repricing the retail debt portfolio introduces interest rate risks and thus impacts spreads.

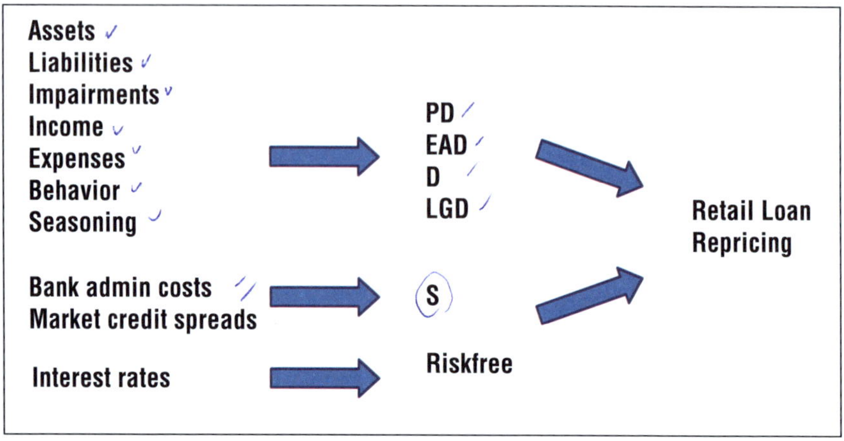

FIGURE 2.3 Retail Credit Risk Map

As noted, it is critical for a bank to understand retail credit risks well, because retail lending is a large component of bank lending and retail credit performance reflects macroeconomic factors, which affect large blocks of similar consumer loan portfolios. Furthermore, some of the drivers of consumer loan valuation also affect consumer deposit behavior. For instance, retail deposit and loan behavior is related: when the retail deposit base shrinks during economic contraction, retail loans also become riskier. This behavioral relationship, which lies at the core of contemporary models to assess interest rate and liquidity risk in banks, is explored in greater detail in *Asset and Liability Management*, another volume in the GARP Financial Risk and Regulation Series. The interaction between retail loans and retail deposits can introduce an additional level of complexity in understanding the drivers of retail credit risk.

2.2 Small and Medium-Sized Enterprise (SME) Credit Risks

SME borrowers range from small businesses to larger international corporations that are considered small by global standards. Many SMEs are family owned or closely held partnerships, where the owners have intimate knowledge of the business but a limited understanding of finance and credit. Owners and managers of SMEs tend to focus on running the business, and, often, as a result, the financial aspects of the business are not prioritized.

There is no widely accepted definition of what is a typical SME credit. One approach is to consider a bank's own definition. For small banks, almost all commercial loans are SME loans, while for larger banks (particularly those that are internationally active), SME loans can be underwritten to borrowers with sales in the millions. From a regulatory perspective, the Basel II Accord differentiates between large corporations and SMEs through sales volume: corporations with consolidated annual sales less than EUR 50 million are considered as SMEs. In many parts of the world, a company with annual sales of EUR 50 million or its equivalent would be considered as a large corporation.

Compared to retail loans that can be analyzed fairly inexpensively using credit scoring and other metrics, SME loan applications have historically relied on manual analysis of financial information. Such information may not always be easily accessible partly due to quality control issues and partly due to limited availability of information. For a small SME loan, manual underwriting—involving the collection and review of financial statements and other labor-intensive work—could take at least one or two days to analyze, at considerable cost.

Given the relatively small amounts involved in SME credit products, the borrower's price sensitivity limiting bank compensation, and the underwriting cost, SME lending has not always been viewed as a profitable venture for the larger banks. In fact, many banks set hard financial and accounting thresholds on the size of potential SME borrowers; those that fall short of such thresholds are frequently not pursued.

The advent of SME scoring systems has enabled credit risk assessments to be determined quickly and reliably and therefore more cheaply. Similar to a retail credit application, the SME applicant's data can be processed through an analytical model which delivers a number (a score or grade) that indicates the associated level of credit risk. In a typical financial institution, neither scoring nor automated underwriting completely replaces manual underwriting, but effective use of these techniques can sharply reduce the number of applications that require further manual review: often by as much as 50–80%.

2.2.1 Credit Scorecards for the SME sector

The benefits of using SME scorecards are significant and have enabled banks to actively manage their exposures to individual SME obligors.

Credit scorecards have enabled banks to reduce the costs and time needed to analyze and underwrite a loan and, due to the risk-based structure embedded in the scorecard, the lending decision is believed to be far more accurate and reliable. Scorecards also help banks analyze their aggregate credit exposures and track the performance of individual credits over the bank's life cycle, and thereby offer more risk-sensitive pricing.

Through automation, banks are able to approve and process a higher loan volume. This increased efficiency has allowed banks to make more loans to SMEs, and to offer financing and other credit services that better serve the specific need of this market segment.

Scorecards provide an effective opportunity to control individual exposures, due to the accuracy and effectiveness of scoring models based on rigorous statistical analysis. In developing countries, where the quality of financial statement information is often unreliable, the use of these scorecards is highly valued.

Through automation and objective procedures, scorecards have removed human bias, at least partially, from the lending decision process. Credit scoring systems only evaluate data found to correlate with future credit performance. This is considered objective decision making, and is one of the Basel II criteria.

Scorecards offer banks the opportunity to focus on questionable loans. Using a scorecard-based credit assessment process allows banks to extend a larger number of loans based on scores and automated decision criteria, instead of on judgmental factors alone. This process has given credit officers the opportunity to concentrate their efforts on reviewing questionable loan requests, on requests for larger amounts, or on existing loans that may be deteriorating. Similarly, extending an existing SME loan that was underwritten using a scorecard can substantially help the bank by correctly assessing the marginal risk of the borrower, and the risk of any new exposure.

2.2.2 Credit Scoring Benefits

Banking supervisors have also observed the advantages of credit scoring models. Accordingly, there is an emerging consensus among leading bank supervisors that correct application of credit scoring methodologies increases the consistency, speed, and accuracy of credit evaluations, while also reducing the associated costs. Furthermore, credit scoring methodologies standardize the bank's analytical approach and so ultimately reduce both personal bias and the use of conflicting heuristics. As a result, the operational risks associated with SME credit underwriting have declined.

Increased standardization not only reduces the cost of underwriting, but also improves the ability to compare the risk and return features of different loans. Credit scoring reduces some of the observed variation in the way risks are assessed among loan officers or by a single loan officer over time.

2.3 Corporate Credit Risks

Qualitatively, corporate credit risk resembles retail and SME risk since valuation is affected by income, asset quality, and macroeconomic factors. However, a critical difference stems from the availability of greater information from the corporate market. The availability of this information can work in a bank's favor because it makes fraud more difficult. In addition, for larger corporations with traded bonds, market-based information about expected loss rates can be inferred from bond prices or their credit-default swap spreads (see Chapter 3). Finally, corporations can be expected to act in their economic best interest, i.e., their shareholders' interest. The inference is that their behavior may be more predictable than the behavior of retail and SME customers who sometimes act irrationally. However, this does not always follow, considering instances where corporations have chosen to selectively default or to accelerate default.

2.3.1 Corporate Loans held by Banks

According the weekly Federal Reserve H.8 release for December 28, 2014, US bank credit held by commercial banks (including foreign banks) amounted to approximately USD 11 trillion in credit; 30% of that was extended to corporate borrowers. The banks held just under USD 1.8 trillion in corporate loans and just over USD 1.6 trillion in loans tied to commercial real estate. Additionally, banks have further corporate credit exposure through their investment activities, e.g., through their counterparty exposures. These latter credit risks may not always be apparent but may amplify a bank's credit risk exposure when considered in aggregate.

2.3.2 Corporate Credit Risk Models

Many banks have developed their own internal rating systems for corporate borrowers. Most of these systems are based on a combination of quantitative and qualitative inputs. In some cases, the bank's own rating scale incorporates inputs obtained from credit rating agencies such as Moody's, S&P, and Fitch. In other cases, when companies are unrated by the credit rating agencies either because of size or other considerations, the bank's internal rating system becomes the sole determining factor for credit risk scoring. For this reason, banks must either develop their own corporate credit models or use a commercially available model.

Broadly speaking, there are two types of corporate credit models, structural models and reduced-form models. Structural models try to determine what factors cause a company to be more or less likely to default on its debt. Ratio-based models are structural in nature as they try to link performance indicators to default probabilities. Reduced-form models start with an assumed or calibrated probability of default, and link its changes over time to firm-specific, industry, or macroeconomic variables. Variations of both types of models are widely used by banks in their efforts to quantify corporate credit risk. The most widely used are discussed next.

2.3.3 Altman's *Z*-Score

One of the earliest credit scoring models was an academic study designed in the 1960's by Professor Edward Altman, known as Altman's Z-score.[2] The model, which was based on a small sample of manufacturing companies in the US where half of the sample defaulted, linked a company's financial performance to an overall credit score.

The *Z*-score is based on the use of financial ratios to predict corporate deterioration. The original model incorporated the following five variables (ratios):

- Working capital to total assets
- Return on total assets
- Sales to total assets
- Equity to debt
- Retained earnings to total assets

The *Z*-score is a weighted sum of these factors that falls between –4 and 1. Financially sound companies generally obtain *Z*-scores above 2.99, while those scoring below 1.81 are in danger. Scores that fall between 2.99 and 1.81 suggest the possibility of financial distress. In Altman's original study of 33 bankrupt companies, *Z*-scores for 95% of these companies pointed to trouble or imminent default.

Although this research is dated and its sample size limited in size and scope, the approach became very popular because of its reliability, scalability, and relative simplicity. Over time, the *Z*-score formula has been changed by

2 Edward Altman, "Financial Ratios, Discriminant Analysis, and the Prediction of Corporate Bankruptcy," *Journal of Finance*, 1968.

Professor Altman and others, but the core of this approach—using the size and relative relationship across accounting ratios—is widely believed to be an accurate predictor of financial distress.

Based on the principles utilized in the design of the Z-score, many others have built competing models that expand the use of this methodology to include privately held firms, firms in highly specific sectors, and firms of a certain asset size, such as SMEs.

2.3.4 Merton's Distance-to-Default Model

Another class of structural models is based on Professor Robert Merton's work on the pricing of corporate debt,[3] in which equity is modeled as a call option on the assets of the firm.

Ownership of equity in a business is similar to owning a call option to buy the business for the value of its liabilities. In other words, the value of the call option reflects and closely follows the value of the equity of the business. When the firm is worth more than its liabilities, then the difference between assets and liabilities should be more or less the value of the company's equity. In this situation, the owner of the business has two options: service the company's creditors as long as the company is worth more than its liabilities, or realize the owner's equity value. However, once the value of the assets is less than the liabilities, the owner may choose not to exercise the option of paying the creditors, and in fact can renege and default on the loan.

Merton and others later refined the use of the option theory combined with default definitions and forward-looking data extracted from the equity markets to derive more dynamic and predictive models for default probability. One widely used Merton model is Moody's CreditEdge which calculates an EDF (expected default frequency). The model uses three drivers to arrive at an approximation of default probability within a specific time horizon.

1. Market value of assets
2. Default point
3. Asset volatility

Note that the model is based on the market value of the assets, not the accounting value. While the market value of all of a company's assets is

3 Robert C Merton, "On the Pricing of Corporate Debt: The Risk Structure of Interest Rates," *The Journal of Finance*, 1974.

not directly observable, these and similar models revert to using a proxy: information that is directly available and observable. To infer the market value of assets and the volatility of assets, these models use observable price information from traded financial instruments, chiefly equity. As noted above, equity behaves like a call option, its value increases when the value of the assets increases and PD falls.

In practice, this dynamic relationship is captured in the distance-to-default measure, which captures the estimated number of standard deviations asset values would have to fall to make default possible. One major advantage of this approach is that it uses updated market information to continuously re-assess the creditworthiness of an organization. One disadvantage of this approach however, is that if market prices change for reasons unrelated to credit quality, the methodology will cause spurious changes in PD estimates.

A summary risk map including corporate credit risk and counterparty risk, is presented in Section 2.4.3.

2.3.5 Credit Rating Agency (CRA) Ratings

Credit rating agencies (CRAs), such as Moody's, S&P, and Fitch, publish credit ratings, measures of the risk that companies will default on their debt securities. CRAs use a combination of qualitative and quantitative analyses to derive their credit ratings and have the benefit of detailed information about each rated company as well as years of data collection and analysis to base their ratings on. Unlike Merton-type models, CRA ratings may include substantial weight from qualitative factors as well as forward-looking information. However, they have much in common with Z-score-type models in terms of using financial ratios to link performance indicators to default probabilities.

Based on its research and analysis of thousands of companies and their financial statements, Moody's[4] has outlined 11 key financial ratios believed to provide a useful and foundational set of metrics for comparative analysis across industries and regions. However, the agency also notes that ratio analysis is only one part of its analytical process and that qualitative and forward-looking considerations are also important.

Moody's metrics are listed in the table below, complemented with the metrics per broad rating category. It should be noted that the Baa category

4 We could easily have chosen S&P or Fitch to present the general conclusions of this section. At this level of abstraction, the rating assessment processes are similar, and the purpose of this section is to show the complex credit rating process rather than to directly or indirectly endorse one approach over another.

is used as the industry guide for the separation of investment-grade and non-investment-grade companies. In its analysis, Moody's finds that for nine of the eleven ratios, there exists a strong monotonic relationship between the ratios and a company's ratings, with leverage and gearing monotonically decreasing with ratings, as expected, and margins, returns, interest coverage, and cash flow coverage increasing with ratings. Only two ratios, capital expenditure (CAPEX)/depreciation and revenue volatility, were not found to be strictly monotonic, but nevertheless provided useful comparative data.

	EBITA / Average Assets	Operating Margin	EBITA Margin	EBITA / Interest Expense	(FFO + InExp) / IntExp
Aaa	20.9%	22.0%	25.1%	28.9	25.4
Aa	12.5%	15.4%	16.2%	16.7	16.6
A	12.1%	14.7%	15.5%	9.3	10.3
Baa	9.8%	13.5%	15.0%	5.5	6.9
Ba	8.7%	11.5%	12.6%	3.3	4.5
B	7.1%	9.2%	10.6%	1.7	2.7
C	3.8%	4.1%	5.7%	0.5	1.4

	Debt / EBITDA	Debt / Book Capitalization	FFO / Debt	Retained Cash Flow / Net Debt	CAPEX / Depreciation	Revenue Volatility
Aaa	0.6	19.3%	133.5%	1.3	1.4	11.2
Aa	1.8	35.3%	48.7%	0.3	1.4	7.3
A	2.0	40.8%	37.9%	0.3	1.4	10.8
Baa	2.7	45.6%	27.5%	0.2	1.3	13.5
Ba	3.5	52.2%	19.7%	0.2	1.3	16.6
B	5.1	67.2%	11.9%	0.1	1.1	17.7
C	7.3	85.3%	4.0%	0.0	0.7	14.8

FIGURE 2.4 Moody's Aggregate Key Financial Metrics, US companies, December 2013

Source: Moody's Financial Metrics™ Key Ratios by Rating and Industry for North American Non-Financial Corporations: December 2013, February 11, 2014.

Figure 2.4 illustrates the large gap between ratios for companies in different rating grades. For example, a Baa-rated company on average achieves a funds-from-operations-to-debt ratio (FFO/Debt) of 27.5% or higher, which is considerably stronger than the 4% achieved on average by a C-rated company but substantially weaker than the 133% achieved by an average Aaa-rated corporate.

Figure 2.5 shows one particular key ratio, interest coverage, Median EBITA (earnings before interest, tax, and amortization of intangibles)/Interest, across the rating grades for different industries in the US. The aggregate median EBITA/Interest for investment-grade (Baa-rated or better) companies is 5.9x or better. However, for companies in the automotive sector, the median ratio is 7.7x and for retail/distribution companies it is only 4.4x. According to Moody's, the evidence suggests that intrinsically more risky industries are required to achieve better credit ratios to obtain a given rating.

		Aaa	Aa	A	Baa	Ba	B	C
Aggregate		28.9	15.1	9.7	5.9	3.5	1.7	0.6
	n=	4	14	94	255	274	300	43
Aerospace & Defense				7.5	5.9	4.8	1.9	0.7
	n=			8	5	14	3	1
Automotive					7.7	5.5	1.8	0.6
	n=			1	4	7	15	2
Chemicals				9.3	6.7	3.2	1.9	0.2
	n=			5	19	17	3	1
Consumer Products			18.3	8.2	5.6	3.5	1.6	0.4
	n=		4	16	44	51	55	6
Energy & Environment		34.2	35.1	8.7	4.4	2.7	1.8	0.0
	n=	1	2	12	55	47	50	5
Healthcare		23.6		15.0	9.0	3.7	1.7	1.2
	n=	1		11	18	9	16	1
Manufacturing			11.9	10.7	9.4	3.2	2.2	0.4
	n=		2	12	24	29	24	4
Media				9.6	5.1	2.8	1.8	1.0
	n=			1	11	15	18	8
Metals & Mining				6.5	6.9	2.8	1.0	-1.3
	n=			1	12	10	15	6
Retail & Distribution			9.3	7.3	5.3	3.7	1.4	1.1
	n=		1	7	20	18	31	2
Services		22.9		7.3	6.5	4.5	1.7	
	n=	1		1	4	18	25	
Telecommunications		9.6	59.5	19.6	6.0	3.9	1.4	0.4
	n=	1	3	16	32	34	36	4
Transportation			3.3	9.2	5.8	4.3	1.8	0.6
	n=		2	3	7	5	9	3

FIGURE 2.5 2013 Median EBITA/Interest Expense for US Corporates (Moody's)
Source: Moody's Financial Metrics™ Key Ratios by Rating and Industry for North American Non-Financial Corporations: December 2013, February 11, 2014.

The ratios in Figure 2.5 reflect US data; it is interesting to consider geographic impacts. Comparing the US ratios to the global ratios produced by Moody's shows that the median EBITA/Interest globally for a Baa company is 5.5x versus 5.9x in the US. In terms of geographic and industry impacts, the global median ratio for a Baa in the automotive sector is 8.4x compared to 7.7x in the US, but retail/distribution globally is 4.8x compared with 5.3x in the US.

		Aaa	Aa	A	Baa	Ba	B	C
Aggregate		28.9	16.7	9.3	5.5	3.3	1.7	0.5
	n=	4	30	169	425	424	434	61
Aerospace & Defense				7.7	6.0	4.8	1.9	0.7
	n=			9	8	14	3	1
Automotive			20.9	9.8	8.4	4.9	1.8	0.6
	n=		1	6	10	15	18	2
Chemicals			129.7	9.3	6.7	3.1	1.9	0.8
	n=		1	13	32	22	9	2
Consumer Products			15.5	8.7	5.4	3.3	1.7	0.5
	n=		5	27	69	71	80	10
Energy & Environment		34.2	23.5	8.3	4.6	3.0	1.8	0.5
	n=	1	5	15	80	60	57	7
Healthcare		23.6	42.8	15.0	8.1	3.6	1.7	1.2
	n=	1	3	17	20	13	17	1
Manufacturing			8.8	9.2	6.0	3.0	2.1	0.1
	n=		5	30	45	63	60	5
Media				9.6	5.2	2.7	1.7	1.0
	n=			1	24	21	24	8
Metals & Mining				6.5	6.2	2.5	2.0	-0.5
	n=			3	27	26	35	9
Retail & Distribution			6.7	7.0	4.8	3.4	1.3	1.1
	n=		2	12	31	29	38	2
Services		22.9		7.3	6.0	4.5	1.6	
	n=	1		5	9	24	28	
Telecommunications		42.7	49.1	17.6	5.9	3.8	1.5	0.6
	n=	1	4	28	53	53	48	9
Transportation			4.2	9.2	2.8	2.6	1.6	0.5
	n=		4	3	17	13	17	5

FIGURE 2.6 2013 Median EBITA/Interest Expense for Global Corporates according to Moody's

Source: Moody's Financial Metrics™ Key Ratios by Rating and Industry for Global Non-Financial Corporations: December 2013, February 11, 2014.

2.3.6 Limitations of Corporate Credit Risk Models

Academics, statisticians, and credit risk management professionals across the world continue to test, challenge, and seek to refine these models. Nevertheless, as with any model, it is important to understand areas of possible weakness so as to be able to adequately judge the output.

Accounting information
It is important to note that the Generally Accepted Accounting Principles (GAAP) differ across the world. For example, US GAAP permits the use of the last-in-first-out (LIFO) method of inventory measurement but International Financial Reporting Standards (IFRS) do not. Under IFRS, development costs are capitalized but under US GAAP such costs must be expensed as incurred. Differences such as these can result in a misleading comparative analysis, unless adjustments are made to the underlying financial statements to smooth out such differences. In addition, the financial information provided by companies reflects accounting considerations and policies (such as revenue and expense recognition or depreciation policies) that the company has chosen, and these accounting considerations may be fundamentally different across companies even when they are active in the same business and in the same accounting jurisdiction. Finally, by the time a company files its annual report, its credit profile may already be at least three months out of date.

Off-Balance-Sheet Commitments
The use of off-balance-sheet financing, such as operating leases executed through sale and leaseback transactions, may distort a company's financial ratios in terms of leverage or debt capacity and its apparent ability to service such debt.

Through-the-cycle approach of CRAs
The importance of understanding the business cycle is a fundamental part of the corporate analysis undertaken in the underwriting credit process. CRAs also seek to understand the effect of the business cycle on a company and its default risk. However, CRAs typically try to rate "through the business cycle," to consider a company's performance across a business cycle and rate it accordingly. By contrast, rating a company at a point in time, say, at the top of the market or the bottom of the market, will likely produce dramatically different probabilities of default and conflicting output

compared to the CRAs. See Chapter 4 for more discussion of through-the-cycle and point-in-time models.

Timeliness of CRA Ratings

In their ratings of companies and securities, the CRAs seek to deliver accurate and stable opinions of default risk. The element of stability is important to understand because CRAs are reluctant to change a rating if there is a risk of reversing that rating in a short time. By contrast, markets react immediately to new information and it is often the case that the market will price credit information into securities prices before the CRA ratings actually change. Therefore, credit analysts are advised to also track market risk indicators such as bond or CDS prices.

2.3.7 Reduced-Form Models

Introduced by Jarrow and Turnbull (1992, 1995), the reduced-form model starts with an assumed or calibrated probability of default and links its changes over time to firm-specific, industry, or macroeconomic variables. The underlying premise of the model is that corporate default may happen at any time and be triggered by many different factors. As it allows more factors to affect the probability of default than a Merton model, the reduced-form model is considered more flexible than the Merton model. It also allows for a variety of time horizons. Commercial providers (see Chapter 3) such as Kamakura and CreditRisk+ have developed reduced-form credit risk models.

2.4 Counterparty Credit Risks

In addition to the possibility of corporate default on loans, banks need to be concerned with the possibility that corporations will default on obligations created by their trading positions. For example, if a bank enters a gold forward swap with a gold company (the company sells gold forward with delivery and/or payment to be made sometime at a future date), and gold prices rise, the bank is exposed to non-performance by the gold company to the extent its position is under-collateralized. Similarly, the exposure to interest rate and foreign exchange rate swap transactions can rapidly change in value, and it may become impossible for the swap counterparty to make contractual payments.

This risk is similar to corporate credit risk, but is different in several important ways. In this section, we discuss these differences and explain the tools banks use to assess counterparty risk.

2.4.1 How counterparty credit differs from corporate credit

These are the main features of counterparty credit risk assessment that differ from traditional credit risk assessment:

- Exposures can often be netted
- EAD is variable, unknown in advance, and driven by market risk factors
- EAD may be negatively correlated to PD
- Counterparty risk creates a two-way credit exposure
- Collateral arrangements are often dynamic in nature

Exposures can often be netted

If a counterparty is subject to a netting agreement, the amounts due to the bank or counterparty in default are simply added up, with positive exposures offsetting negative exposures. Without netting, each trade must be considered as if it were from a separate counterparty, since in the event of counterparty default, the bank would have to pay on losing positions while not collecting on winning positions.

In analyzing the effects of netting, the bank must understand the legal rules related to netting. Simply because there is a "nettable" exposure against a counterparty, may not mean that netting is possible without specifically adjusting for differences in recoverability.

Variable EAD

At the point of counterparty default, a bank loses the mark-to-market value of its position if positive, and captures the collateral value. The EAD is therefore given by the higher of: (a) the difference between mark-to-market value and collateral value and (b) zero. For this reason, exposure behaves like a call option with the underlying value being the mark-to-market value of the asset and the strike price being the value of the collateral.

Negative relationship between EAD and PD

Under normal lending circumstances, when an obligor's financial health deteriorates, a bank can expect that the obligor's PD and LGD have increased. This occurs because asset value (used for LGD) tends to decline as income declines (affecting PD). In counterparty credit risk assessment, the opposite effect is sometimes observed. For example, in the case of the gold company above, the gold company is in a losing position on the swap when its asset value is higher due to higher gold prices. Therefore, even though the company's EAD is increasing, its PD and LGD are falling.

Two-way credit exposure
If a bank's mark-to-market value becomes negative, its counterparty has credit exposure to the bank. Therefore, bank counterparties need to make the same assessments as banks when they enter into trading arrangements.

EXAMPLE

Bank C enters into an interest rate swap with counterparty A whereby Bank C pays A a fixed rate of 4%; if market rates are 5% for five more years, the PV is 4.32% of the notional principal amount (NPA). This is positive credit risk.

However, if Bank C is paying 4% when the market rate is 3% for five more years, the PV is negative 4.58% of the NPA. This is negative credit risk, in other words, Counterparty A has credit exposure to Bank C.

Dynamic collateral
Depending on the terms of trade, a bank may be able to ask for additional collateral when a trade moves in its favor, and terminate the trade if the counterparty fails to supply the collateral. While this does not eliminate credit exposure, dynamic collateral can mitigate exposure significantly.

2.4.2 Assessing Counterparty Credit

All the traditional credit analysis tools described in the corporate credit risk section can also be used to assess counterparty risk. For some banks, credit risk management policy will be primarily focused on counterparty credit risk. To determine a bank's potential exposures, the risk management function may employ a series of different approaches to reflect the inherent characteristics of the financial instruments as well as the bank's counterparties. For instance, for fixed income and foreign exchange derivatives, as well as credit risk management, a bank might use Monte Carlo simulation while for the bank's securities financing, it might use a historical simulation.

Figure 2.7 demonstrates an example of a one-year swap with constant underlying volatility. The peak exposure is reached in about four months. Banks use this measure, the potential future exposure (PFE) together with a

PFE limit, to control their credit exposure to any single counterparty. PFEs may also be aggregated to determine bankwide credit risk to counterparty.

Over time, the EAD of the swap first increases with increasing future interest rate uncertainty, but then falls as the swap amortizes, the maturity shortens, and the future interest rate uncertainty is reduced.

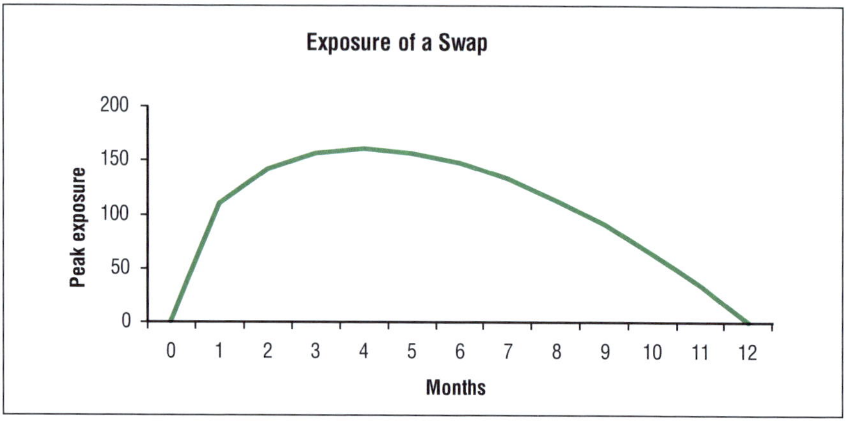

FIGURE 2.7: Swap Exposure

EXAMPLE

If a bank has counterparty loans outstanding of USD 500 million, a PFE of USD 80 million, and an overall credit limit of USD 600 million, the bank can either increase its lending lines by USD 20 million or increase its trading activity, as long as the PFE stays under USD 600 million.

Banks often use these concepts to convert their counterparty exposures into loan-equivalent exposures (i.e., fictitious loans that would have the same expected EAD as the counterparty's swap portfolio). This is a complex process which requires an analysis of several key assumptions and it is beyond the scope of this discussion. Once converted according to EAD, the counterparty's PD and LGD estimates would apply to both the actual debt positions and to the counterparty credit exposures.

2.4.3 Summary of Corporate Credit and Counterparty Risk Drivers

Corporate obligations to banks are repriced in the same way as retail credit obligations. Changes in a firm's characteristics, especially its performance, leverage, and income, cause the PD estimate to change over time, often through a change in the credit rating. The EAD is either the amount of the debt or, in the case of counterparty obligations, an estimate based on what the exposure could be. The drivers of corporate LGD were discussed in Chapter 1.

As a bank reprices its loans, bonds, and counterparty obligations, it gains a better understanding of the value of its assets and the risk drivers that cause values to fluctuate.

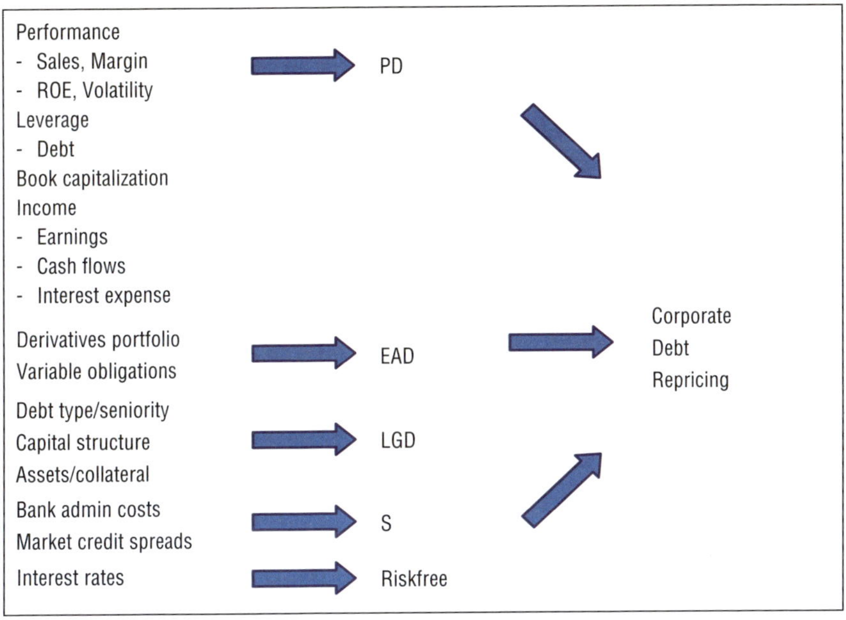

FIGURE 2.8 SME, Corporate, and Counterparty Credit Risk Map

2.5 Sovereign Credit Risk

A sovereign borrower differs from corporate borrowers and other counterparties by virtue of the fact that sovereigns cannot go bankrupt: bankruptcy is governed by national law and there is no entity to take over the assets of a government and redistribute them to creditors. When a government is in financial distress, its debts are typically renegotiated and restructured. However, there have been cases where sovereigns have defaulted on their debts.

Sovereign risk can arise from actions taken by sovereign governments or other parties, or from macroeconomic factors that affect the values of securities or contracts within a sovereign jurisdiction.

Sovereign credit losses can be triggered by any of the following:

- Financial health of a country
- War and warlike events
- Expropriation (explicit or implicit, for example, through tax increases)
- Discriminatory actions of one country against another
- Currency inconvertibility
- Transfer delays
- Rescheduling process outcomes

A bank encounters sovereign risk through its holding of sovereign debt and holdings of foreign currency-denominated or foreign-originated corporate liabilities. Also, to the extent that a bank deals with foreign governments, and with foreign banks and non-bank corporations, sovereign risk becomes a component of counterparty credit risk.

The entire premise of sovereign borrowing builds on the ability of a country's government to raise sufficient funds to fully repay debtors either through raising taxes and cutting government expenses, or by monetizing the debt through monetary policy, i.e., printing new currency to repay lenders. Given that governments control taxation, government spending, and monetary policy, they ultimately control debt repayments. Even during times of financial exigency, many investors rely on sovereign debt as an integral component of their investment portfolio.

Furthermore, since most sovereigns do not fully repay the bulk of their debt but refinance it with new borrowings at rates reflective of their current creditworthiness, sovereign debt provides an important benchmark for non-government borrowing.

Typically, sovereign credits are highly rated and considered as reliable, although as Figure 2.9 shows, the proportion of non-investment or speculative grade sovereign borrowers has increased since 2005. The growth in non-investment-grade sovereign borrowing reflects both increasing demand for financing by developing countries and increased investor appetite for higher yielding securities compared to the ultra-low yields available on bonds in advanced countries. However, the inclusion of new ratings from previously unrated countries, particularly in Africa, combined with downward rating migration of some sovereigns, particularly in Europe, has also contributed to the increase in the proportion of non-investment-grade sovereign ratings in recent years. Indeed, prior to the global financial crisis, no advanced economy was rated non-investment grade, but by the end of 2012, four countries—Cyprus, Greece, Ireland, and Portugal—had been downgraded to sub-investment grades, and of those four, by February 2015, only Ireland had managed to regain its investment-grade status.

Rating	1983	1990	1995	2000	2005	2010	2012	2013
Aaa	79%	33%	16%	12%	19%	15%	13%	12%
Aa	21%	28%	25%	15%	7%	15%	12%	12%
A	0%	17%	18%	10%	22%	13%	8%	7%
Baa	0%	8%	18%	21%	14%	18%	26%	24%
Ba	0%	8%	16%	19%	15%	16%	16%	17%
B	0%	6%	5%	19%	17%	23%	22%	21%
Caa_C	0%	0%	0%	4%	5%	1%	3%	7%
Investment grade	100%	86%	78%	59%	63%	61%	59%	55%
Speculative grade	0%	14%	22%	41%	37%	39%	41%	45%

FIGURE 2.9 Rating Distribution of Sovereign Issuers on Selected Dates
Source: Moody's Sovereign Default and Recovery Rates, 1983-2013 (published April 2014)

2.5.1 The Market for Sovereign Credit

Because sovereigns and entities protected by sovereigns cannot be compelled to report data, it is often difficult to get a complete picture of sovereign debt statistics. The best sources are the Bank for International Settlements (BIS), which has the voluntary participation of most central banks, and the International Monetary Fund (IMF), which takes an active role in many sovereign-related activities.

In its 2015 study "Debt and (Not Much) Deleveraging," McKinsey Global Institute calculate that, as of June 2014, the global stock of government debt stood at USD 58 trillion. This represented an increase of USD 25 trillion since 2007, of which USD 19 trillion was in advanced economies and USD 6 trillion in developing countries.

According to the Statistical Annex of the BIS Quarterly Review for December 2014, with a reporting date of June 2014, the international positions of banks by residence of counterparty amounted to USD 34.5 trillion. In other words, the external positions held by reporting banks subject to sovereign risk considerations amounted to USD 34.5 trillion. By nationality, Japanese banks held the largest external position at USD 4.6

trillion, followed by the US at USD 3.9 trillion, the UK at USD 3.9 trillion, France at USD 3.8 trillion, and Germany at USD 3.7 trillion. Most of the cross-border claims were denominated in USD (USD 15.1 trillion) and EUR (USD 10.8 trillion).

From a bank's perspective, exposure to sovereign debt is essential and many banks make extensive use of government securities. Because of their relative safety and liquidity, investment-grade sovereign and government bonds are useful for liquidity risk management. Even if its own government's debt does not have an investment-grade rating, national bank regulators often require a bank to hold government securities on its books. Indeed, recognizing the relatively lower risk of these securities, regulators typically assign low risk ratings to sovereign debt. The Basel framework assigns 0% risk weight for government debt issued by OECD countries. A 0% risk weight implies that the bank is not required to reserve capital against such debt instruments and therefore has more leeway to invest in other, more risky, debt instruments that may optimize the return on its portfolio. Thus, sovereign debt is an integral part of bank holdings, both as a precautionary tool and as a tool to generate income.

2.5.2 Risk factors in Sovereign Credit

Sovereign credit risk results from non-diversifiable country risks affecting all issuers or obligors in a specific country. In other words, risks that cannot be mitigated by portfolio management or other forms of credit enhancement. The key risk factors in sovereign risk stem from political risk such as instability or threats of asset nationalization; institutional risk such as the integrity of the judicial system; financial and economic risks; and event risks resulting from geopolitical tensions or natural disasters.

As is true for any obligor, a qualitative as well as quantitative approach is necessary when analyzing sovereign risks. For sovereign analysis, historical, political, and cultural factors may prove especially important.

With respect to a quantitative approach, there are several sources of data and statistics such as the World Bank and the IMF that the analyst may utilize. In its Statistical Handbook on Country Credit, November 2014, Moody's lists 54 quantitative factors that are used in its sovereign rating process.

Moody's notes that the relevance of specific economic and financial variables can vary according to the country's broad level of development. In its sovereign credit handbook, more detail is provided on macroeconomic variables for advanced countries and more detail on external debt and balance of payment information is included in the tables for developing countries.

The quantitative factors fall into four categories:

1. Economic structure and performance
2. Government finance
3. External payments and debt
4. Monetary, external-vulnerability, and liquidity indicators

Economic structure and performance
This category includes statistics related to GDP, inflation, unemployment, gross investment and saving, exports, and imports. It also includes measures of the openness of the economy and government effectiveness. Overall, it can be expected that countries with strong production, low inflation, low unemployment, high degrees of investment and saving, and a balance of exports to imports will be judged to be more creditworthy than a country that does not exhibit these qualities.

Government finance
These measures include government revenue, expenses, financial balances, and debt as a percentage of GDP, along with a few other measures. If a country's government is well managed, i.e., preferably not using deficit financing, and with a responsible level of debt, it can expect to have a higher credit rating than governments in countries that do not exhibit these qualities.

External payments and debt
These measures include exchange rates, labor costs, current account balance, external debt measures, foreign direct investment, foreign exchange reserves, and measures of the health of domestic banks. These indirect measures of creditworthiness can often illuminate situations where a sovereign passes the basic reporting tests but other investors have lost confidence in the country, as might be illustrated by a fall in foreign direct investment in the country.

Monetary, external vulnerability, and liquidity indicators
These measures include money supply measures, domestic interest rates and credit, an external vulnerability indicator, liquidity ratios, and dollarization ratios (i.e., the degree to which citizens of the country hold outside currency as a hedge against their own sovereign risk).

2.5.3 The Relationship between Sovereign Ratings and Corporate Ratings

Sovereign risk is a key consideration in analyzing the credit risk of non-sovereign borrowers. Many market participants consider the sovereign's credit rating as the de facto ceiling for credit ratings for obligors and obligations from that country.

However, sovereign risk is often amplified for certain obligors such as banks or financial institutions, and for government-related entities or state-owned enterprises such as utilities. This was seen during the European sovereign debt crisis where countries such as Italy imposed additional taxes on utilities and energy companies in a bid to strengthen fiscal reserves, but the utilities were also negatively impacted by declines in manufacturing output and lower residential usage as a result of the economic crisis.

Nevertheless, there are some examples where a corporate issuer is rated higher than its sovereign. In such cases, the corporate is judged to have sufficient operating and financial strengths to be able to mitigate the risks of operating in that particular country; and it typically demonstrates geographic diversification, having assets and cash flow generation in other countries.

EXAMPLE

In February 2015, Fage International SA, a Greek yogurt manufacturer and marketer, was rated B by Standard & Poor's and B3 by Moody's Investors Service, in both cases with a stable outlook. At the same time, Moody's rated rated Greece as Caa1, with the rating under review for possible downgrade, while Standard & Poor's rated Greece as B–, with Credit-Watch negative. The resilience and strength of Fage's international operations, and its US business in particular, enabled the company to weather the serious contraction in the Greek dairy market that followed the Greek sovereign crisis of 2012. As a result, it was able to receive a higher rating than its sovereign.

2.5.4 Sovereign Default

As outlined at the beginning of the section, a sovereign may default on its obligations but unlike a corporation, a sovereign cannot be put into liquidation or administration; therefore a solution has to be negotiated rather than imposed by a legal court. Occasionally a sovereign has unilaterally defaulted without good-faith negotiations with its creditors, as did Argentina in 2002. However, more frequently, there is tremendous political will to resolve a sovereign debt crisis as quickly and calmly as possible.

Reducing the likelihood of sovereign default becomes an international political problem because of the ultimate owners of sovereign debt. Banks hold most sovereign debt, and those holdings are financed by deposits. As discussed, most banks use sovereign debt as a part of their asset and liquidity management portfolios. Because sovereign debt is considered relatively low risk, banks pledge sovereign debt for various repo transactions that finance lending and commercial operations.

In effect, using sovereign debt as collateral, banks can monetize their assets and transform a low-yielding but secure asset, through leverage and asset substitution, into a higher-yielding but riskier asset. Moreover, when computing risk-based capital standards, banks benefit from the lower risk-weights sovereign debt carries; sovereign debt can carry risk-weights as low as 0%. Any deterioration of sovereign-debt credit quality would raise the risk-weight from the 0% floor to higher levels. Sovereign credit rating downgrades would invariably lead to the unwinding of many repo transactions as such transactions are structured on a certain base-line credit rating for the repo'd asset. As a result of these two possible subsequent developments, banks would be forced to reserve more capital against these sovereign loans.

According to Moody's, the causes of sovereign default can generally be grouped into four categories: unsustainably high debt burden (e.g., Pakistan or Greece), political instability culminating in unwillingness to pay (Venezuela and Russia), a banking crisis (Ecuador), and chronic economic stagnation (Argentina and Ukraine).

Between 1998 and 2013, 14 countries with sovereign debt rated by Moody's defaulted, as Figure 2.10 shows.

Default Date	Country	Total Defaulted Debt (USD Millions)
July 1998	Venezuela	270
August 1998	Russia	72,709
September 1998	Ukraine	1,271
July 1999	Pakistan	1,627
August 1999	Ecuador	6,604
January 2000	Ukraine	1,064
November 2001	Argentina	82,268
June 2002	Moldova	145
May 2003	Uruguay	5,744
July 2003	Nicaragua	320
April 2005	Dominican Republic	1,622
December 2006	Belize	242
June 2008	Nicaragua	296
December 2008	Ecuador	3,210
February 2010	Jamaica	7,900
March 2012	Greece	261,478
September 2012	Belize	547
December 2012	Greece	42,076
February 2013	Jamaica	9,100
July 2013	Cyprus	1,311

FIGURE 2.10 Moody's-Rated Sovereign Bond Defaults since 1998
Source: Sovereign Default and Recovery Rates, 1983-2013, Moody's Investors Service, April 11, 2014.

The definition of default is important. The simplest definition of default is a missed payment of interest or principal. For parties to a CDS contract, the definition of a default or a credit event is especially relevant. Credit rating agencies typically include distressed exchanges or debt restructurings in their definitions of default. Such distressed exchanges include offering creditors a new or restructured debt or security, possibly with a maturity extension, which enables the obligor to avoid an actual payment default but represents a diminished return to the creditor. Prior to the Greek debt exchange in 2012 (see Section 2.5.6) there was confusion as to whether or not it would constitute a credit event for CDS; it did.

Debt restructurings are a common mechanism to resolve sovereign debt crises. Such restructurings typically provide maturity extensions and interest reduction but only a nominal reduction on debt, thereby alleviating short-term liquidity issues but not resolving unsustainable debt burdens. This largely explains why six of the 14 countries listed in Figure 2.10 have defaulted more than once. The fact that sovereign creditworthiness typically remains very low for several years after a default or debt restructuring and market access is frequently impaired can also lead to subsequent defaults.

Recovery rates on defaulted sovereign bond issuers tend to exhibit a wide variety of outcomes given the variation in the causes for default in the first place. Figure 2.11 provides recovery rates for defaulted sovereigns from 1998 onwards as calculated by 30-day post-default trading prices (where available) and also by the discounted ratio of the value of the old securities to the value of the new securities received in exchange. Where there are large differences between the two estimates, it is largely due to timing differences between when a default or debt exchange was announced compared to when it was effected.

Year of Default	Defaulting Country	Average Trading Price** (% Of PAR)	PV Ratio Of Cash Flows*** (Ratio In %)
1998	Russia	18	50
1999	Pakistan	52	65
1999	Ecuador	44	60
2000	Ukraine	69	60
2000	Ivory Coast*	18	NA
2001	Argentina	27	30
2002	Moldova	60	95
2003	Uruguay	66	85
2003	Nicaragua	NA	50
2004	Grenada*	65	NA
2005	Dominican Republic	95	95
2006	Belize	76	NA
2008	Seychelles*	30	NA
2008	Ecuador	28	NA
2010	Jamaica	90	80
2012	Greece	24	29
2012	Greece	37	40
2012	Belize	40	65
2013	Cyprus	NA	100
2013	Jamaica	NA	89
Issuer-Weighted Recovery Rates		49	66
Value-Weighted Recovery Rates		26	43

* Not rated by Moody's at the time of default;
** 30-day post-default price or distressed exchange trading price;
*** Ratio of the present value of cash flows received as a result of the distressed exchange versus those initially promised, discounted using yield to maturity immediately prior to default.

FIGURE 2.11: Recovery Rates on a Sample of Defaulted Sovereign Bond Issuers
Source: Sovereign Default and Recovery Rates, 1983-2013, Moody's Investors Service, April 11, 2014.

2.5.5 The European Sovereign Debt Crisis

The European sovereign debt crisis began in 2009 shortly after the collapse in the Icelandic banking system. At the end of July 2008, three Icelandic banks had foreign debt in excess of EUR 42 billion, compared to Iceland's GDP of EUR 8.5 billion. In September 2008, after the collapse of Lehman Brothers, the interbank market froze, adversely affecting the Icelandic banks' ability to keep their international banking networks adequately funded.

The three banks were placed into receivership and the Icelandic government sought and received emergency funding of approximately EUR 9 billion from the International Monetary Fund, European Union, Nordic countries, and elsewhere. In addition, the Icelandic government enacted austerity measures, devalued its currency, and enforced strict capital controls.

The Icelandic crisis led to a collapse in creditor confidence in the robustness of other European banking systems and economies such as Ireland, Portugal, and Greece. In Ireland, the sovereign crisis was prompted by a banking crisis similar to Iceland's. However, unlike in the Icelandic crisis, in the Irish crisis, the Irish government stepped in to rescue its banks. In September 2008, the Irish government issued an unlimited guarantee in favor of six Irish banks that were overexposed to the property market and in danger of collapse after Lehman Brother's demise and the ensuing liquidity crisis. However, the cost of the bank rescue was such that the Irish government itself needed to be bailed out by a consortium comprising the IMF, the European Commission, and the European Central Bank, nicknamed the "Troika," and others in late 2010 for EUR 85 billion. The bailout came with demands for adherence to a strict austerity program and structural reforms. However, Ireland benefits from being a small, open economy with a corporate tax regime that supports export-led GDP growth. The country exited the bailout program in December 2013 and its investment-grade rating was reinstated by the credit rating agencies in 2014.

In late 2009, a newly elected Greek government revised calculations of the Greek government deficit from 6% to 13% of GDP (the Maastricht limit for inclusion in the Euro was 3%). In early 2010, the Greek government admitted to having difficulties servicing its debt. The deficit had increased to 14% of GDP and government debt of EUR 216 billion equated to roughly 120% of GDP. In order to receive substantial financing from the Troika during 2010–12, the Greek government agreed to wide-ranging austerity measures, structural reform, and a debt exchange with private-sector bondholders with the objective of reducing its indebtedness. The debt exchange was and remains the largest on record; the government offered to exchange EUR 205.6 billion of existing Greek government debt for newly issued Greek Government Bonds (GGBs) and other considerations, with a plan to reduce debt by EUR 110 billion. In December 2012, the Greek government bought back EUR 31.9 billion of the new GGBs for EUR 11.29 billion, representing a net present value loss for creditors of over 60% and a second default.

In February 2015, Greece was again in troubled negotiations with the Troika as its bailout deal neared expiry. Greece's newly elected government claimed that the austerity measures, structural reforms, and privatizations demanded by the Troika were unworkable and that full repayment of its debts was unfeasible. For its part, the Troika refused to countenance any dilution of its previous requirements, including repayment in full, raising the possibility of a Greek exit from the Euro. Discussions with the Troika continued during the summer of 2015, and eventually in mid-July a provisional agreement was reached between the leaders of the other Eurozone countries to provide a third bailout program to Greece.

2.5.6 Summary of Sovereign Credit Risk Drivers

Sovereign credit risk may occur as a result of actions of a country itself or as a result of outside influences, such as economic sanctions or actions by other countries, or as a result of macroeconomic factors, such as oil or gas price volatility.

Most banks use sovereign debt as part of their asset and liquidity management portfolios, and, because sovereign debt is considered relatively low risk, banks pledge sovereign debt for various repo transactions that finance lending and commercial operations.

Though relatively rare, sovereigns can and do default, typically requiring a debt restructuring or exchange for longer-dated maturities, interest rate relief, and/or a reduction on the absolute amount of debt.

Typically, sovereign default is caused by unsustainable debt burdens, political instability, a banking crisis, and chronic economic stagnation. As a result, recovery rates on defaulted sovereign debt can vary widely.

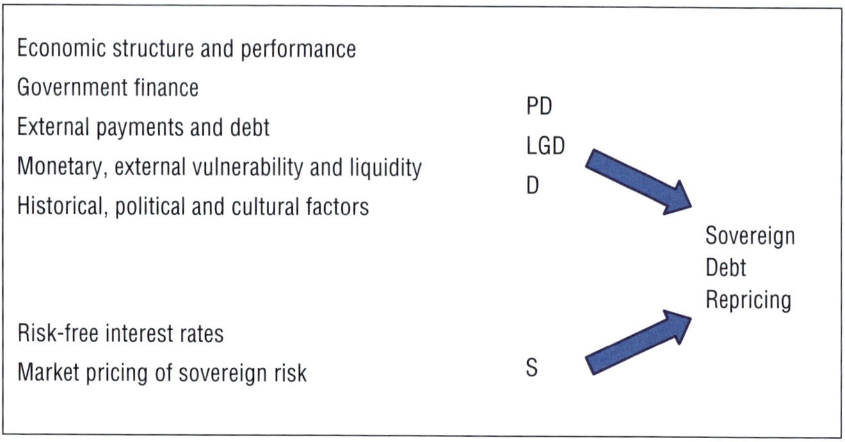

FIGURE 2.12: Sovereign Credit Risk Map

2.6 Summary

This chapter proposes a common credit risk assessment framework that is applicable to retail, corporate, and sovereign credit repricing risk.

Retail credit risk

- US consumers had USD 3.3 trillion in non-real-estate debt outstanding in December 2014.
- Consumer credit quality is frequently estimated by consumer credit reporting bureaus.
- Credit scores are driven by payment history, indebtedness, new credit applications, and the length of the credit history.
- Banks use these scores to determine estimates of PD and LGD.

Corporate credit risk

- Corporate credit risk can be divided into the risk of credit products (loans or lines of credit) and counterparty risk (receivables from derivative positions, repos, or margin lending).
- In the US, banks held USD 10.8 trillion in corporate credit exposures in December 2014.
- Corporate credit risk is normally assessed from corporate credit risk models, based on Altman's *Z*-Score, Merton's distance-to-default, or from credit-rating agencies.

- Credit ratings are intended to summarize information to draw conclusions about both PD and LGD.

Counterparty credit risk

- Counterparty credit risk is similar to corporate credit risk, with a few exceptions.
- Counterparty credit risk refers to the inability to realize gains in a contract with a counterparty due to its default.
- The EAD is variable due to fluctuations in swap valuations.
- The EAD can be negatively correlated to PD.
- Counterparty risk is often two-way.
- Dynamic collateral provisions often reduce counterparty risk considerably.
- PFE, or potential future exposure, is a means to determine EAD for a swap counterparty.

Sovereign credit risk

- According to the BIS, banks globally held USD 34.5 trillion in exposures subject to sovereign credit risk in June 2014.
- Sovereign credit losses can be triggered by the financial health of a country, war and warlike events, expropriation (explicit or implicit through tax increases), discriminatory actions of one country against another, currency inconvertibility, transfer delays, and rescheduling process outcomes.
- Quantitative sovereign credit risk factors include economic structure and performance, government finance, external payments, debt and monetary factors, external vulnerability, and liquidity indicators.
- Qualitative factors include historical, cultural, and political considerations.
- Sovereign debt defaults occur infrequently, but when they occur their effects can be substantial. Sovereign creditworthiness typically remains weak for a number of years and sovereigns may find themselves locked out of the capital markets for lengthy periods.
- Sovereign defaults typically lead to a renegotiation of debt involving maturity extensions, lower interest coupons, and reduction in absolute debt.

CHAPTER 3

Credit Risk Portfolio Management

This chapter considers how a bank aggregates credit information across multiple and diverse obligors to understand and manage its overall credit risk exposure. Aggregate exposure is critical for every loan officer and credit risk manager from the most junior credit analyst to the senior members of the bank's management and board. What is important is not the individual credit exposure, but rather the collective credit exposures in the bank's credit portfolio. A group of good credit decisions can still produce a poor portfolio while a well-structured portfolio can survive poor credit decisions. The precipitous drop in oil prices from 2014 to early 2015 (Brent crude oil fell from USD 114 per barrel in June 2014 to a low of USD 46 per barrel in January 2015), as well as impact of the economic sanctions imposed on Russia around the same time, brought the issue of aggregate exposure even more to the fore as financial institutions considered the impact of events such as these on their various portfolios.

On completion of this chapter the reader will have an improved understanding of:

- The importance of aggregate rather than individual credit exposures.
- The evolution of credit risk management from a proprietary bank-led process to an increasingly transparent discipline.

- Different types of default correlation, for example common risk factors or the possibility of group behavior and the use by banks of copula-type approaches to simulate correlations among obligor defaults.
- Key portfolio measures of credit risk such as EL (i.e., PD × LGD), UL, and credit value-at-risk (CVaR).
- The management of credit risk portfolios, including the use of aggregate risk exposures, returns, the efficient frontier, portfolio stability, risk governance, and concentration risk.
- The use of securitization and credit derivatives as risk management tools.
- The use of credit portfolio models that are produced by commercial vendors or internally developed by banks and the different model forms and structures.
- The operation of specialized workout units that deal with problem assets, have extensive experience in dealing with a wide variety of distressed borrowers, and pursue a number of remedies.
- Asset management companies or aggregator banks that offer to manage banks' non-performing assets.
- The importance of credit risk reporting, using JPMorgan Chase as an example.
- The use of external credit and loan reviews as part of the credit portfolio management process conducted by supervisors or by banks themselves.

3.1 Credit Risk Management

Historically, banks have been characterized as safe and solid institutions whose primary role is to provide credit[5] by:

- Extending credit
- Making profitable investments
- Serving the credit needs of their clients and communities

Over time, the composition of bank credit portfolios has changed. For instance, in the US, the importance of real estate lending has increased while agricultural lending declined, as shown in Figure 3.1.

5 "Loan Portfolio Management, Comptroller's Handbook," US Office of the Comptroller of the Currency, April 1998

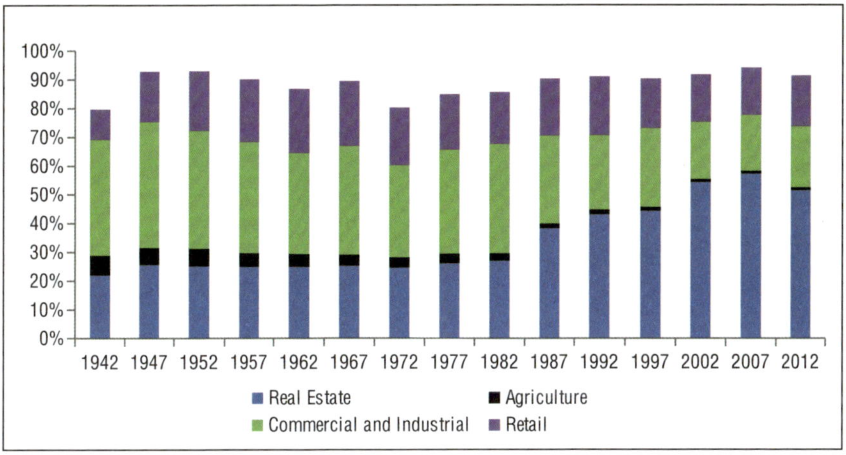

FIGURE 3.1 Composition of US Bank Loan Portfolios 1940–2013
Source: Historical Statistics on Banking provided by the US Federal Deposit Insurance Corporation, www.fdic.gov.

The perception of safety and soundness has grown over time and, for the banking system as a whole, confidence that individual banks are operated safely, soundly, and prudently has evolved as a truly essential feature. However, recent banking history in the developed world has highlighted banking vulnerabilities. Specifically, most of the recent problems that came to the surface during the global financial crisis centered on the quality of banks assets and, in particular, the management of their credit risk portfolios.

Credit risk management is the business of monitoring, measuring, and managing exposures. It requires an understanding of the causes of default or non-performance.

3.1.1 Evolution of Credit Risk Management

We know that banks fail for a variety of reasons, but poor management of credit risk exposures remains the core reason. When a borrower becomes unwilling or unable to repay a loan, that loan becomes a distressed (potentially worthless) asset on the bank's balance sheet. Over the past two decades, banks have broadly adopted the discipline of credit risk management as a result of three significant developments.

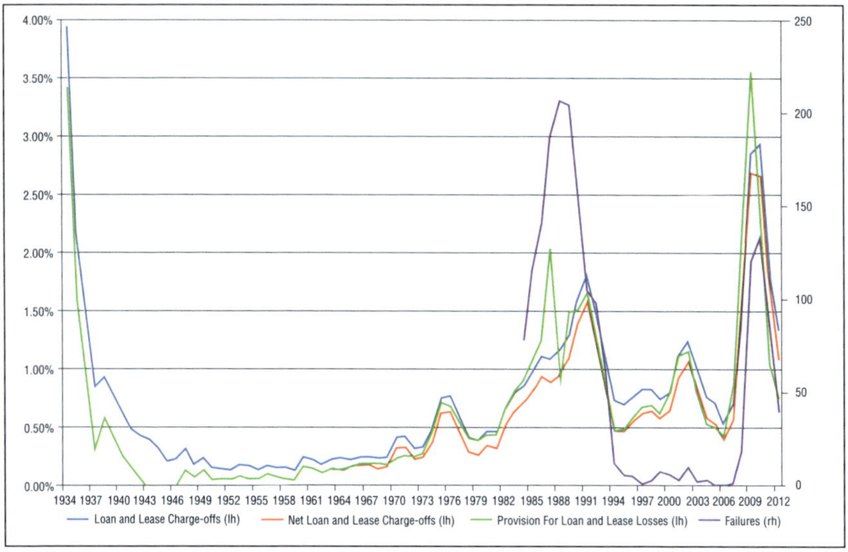

FIGURE 3.2 Credit Risk Measures and Number of Failed Banks in the US
Source: Historical Statistics on Banking provided by the US Federal Deposit Insurance Corporation, www.fdic.gov.

First, because banks had relied upon a code of confidentiality for every aspect of their business, they considered their credit- and portfolio-risk management skills and systems to be proprietary. Although each bank believed that its risk management infrastructure provided a competitive edge, this competitive advantage dissipated quickly with increasing loan product complexity, competition between banks, and the desire to price loans competitively.

Second, as a result of the pioneering work of Edward Altman and Robert Merton, credit risk management received increasing attention from the academic community. This interest was also shared by banks and policy makers. Increasing complexity in lending required increasingly sophisticated risk management approaches. Altman's *Z*-Score and Merton's structural model (Chapter 2) became widely adopted and used in various commercially available as well as proprietary credit models.

Third, with the exception of information provided by the credit rating agencies, the data relevant to analyzing the efficiency of credit risk management—performance of individual loans over a long time—had not been readily available. Banks had to rely on their own historical experiences and data, and could not compare the efficacy of their credit risk management tools with those of other banks, as banks were not interested in sharing this information. However, as banks became more concerned with the usefulness of models, rather than with their proprietary nature, and the usefulness of models increased with academic attention, more disciplined credit risk management became the goal.

These significant developments were also codified in the Basel I Accord. This framework sought to create an internationally valid and commonly applicable regulatory standard by harmonizing bank capital levels and improving the overall safety and soundness of individual banks. Initially, the scope was on credit risk and the level of capital needed to support that risk and it succeeded in establishing a globally valid framework for credit risk management, one which could be applied to any jurisdiction that implemented the Accord's recommendations. When implementing the Accord, most banks realized that they needed to improve their credit risk management policies and procedures.

Another concern was concentration risk. While banks were aware of their highly concentrated loan portfolios, the implications of following such a strategy were not fully appreciated. Consequently, many banking supervisors were not able to appropriately evaluate the overall risk of these portfolios.

3.1.2 The Evolution of Modern Portfolio Theory

The 1990s was a time of major structural change in banks and, in particular, changes to banks' credit risk evaluation processes and methodologies. With the aid of new qualitative analysis techniques and the use of robust quantitative models of analysis, banks soon began to analyze, quantify, and predict their levels of individual and portfolio credit risk.

Driven primarily by the banks' own desire to better understand their risks and partly due to a better assessment of the available capital to support their aggregate credit exposures, a number of new credit-portfolio management methods evolved. By first developing and then refining and recalibrating various default-risk models, banks developed procedures to price risk and calculate the associated capital adequacy. In doing so, banks soon realized the benefits to be gained from a structured and quantitative approach to analyzing individual credits and their aggregate exposures, i.e., reduced capital requirements.

In addition to the new risk management approaches, banks realized that these advanced techniques also created additional business opportunities. Many banks started to engage in securitization and later, by creating increasingly sophisticated credit derivatives, a secondary markets in loans, distressed trading, and other credit risk-related products. All of these products enabled banks to effectively manage many aspects of their credit risk.

3.2 Correlation in Credit Analysis

Early models of credit analysis assumed that a default by one obligor was independent of the default of any other obligor. This assumption was analytically convenient, because it facilitated the development of relatively simple formulas for the determination of portfolio credit risk. However, in practice this was not a good assumption, because there are several factors that can cause several obligors to default at once.

Common risk factors may be harming several obligors with exposures to similar risk factors at once. For example, if the price of crude oil increases, the probability of default for all plastics manufacturers increases as plastics are typically derived from crude oil and other hydrocarbons. If the price of gas decreases, the probability of default for sovereigns such as Russia which rely on revenues from gas exports increases. Similarly, the probability of default for gas-field-services companies increases as lower gas prices may result in fewer drilling projects.

Obligors may exhibit group or herd behavior. Consider the US airline industry where many companies have filed for Chapter 11 (corporate default court proceedings in the US). Upon emergence from Chapter 11, defaulted airlines have reduced debt burdens, and therefore lowered borrowing costs, and have typically arranged better terms with labor unions, making them a formidable competitive force. This may spur other airlines to also consider defaulting.

As these examples show, realistic portfolio credit models must be able to incorporate correlated behaviors in default. In some cases, the default of one obligor can be negatively correlated to the other. This depends on the conditions and strategies of the industry and sector where the business operates. For example, if one packaging company finds itself in financial distress and defaults on its obligations, the prospects for another firm in the business may be better because of reduced competition, implying a lower risk of default. Regardless of the nature of default correlation, banks must characterize correlation in order to understand the aggregate portfolio credit risks.

3.2.1 Common Factors

Chapter 2 discussed the various factors driving an individual obligor's probability of default (PD) and loss given default (LGD). These factors are primarily income and asset considerations. Therefore, any macroeconomic factor that broadly affects income measures or asset valuations will affect large portions of the credit portfolio. Consider the risk map used in Chapter 2 for two different retail obligors.

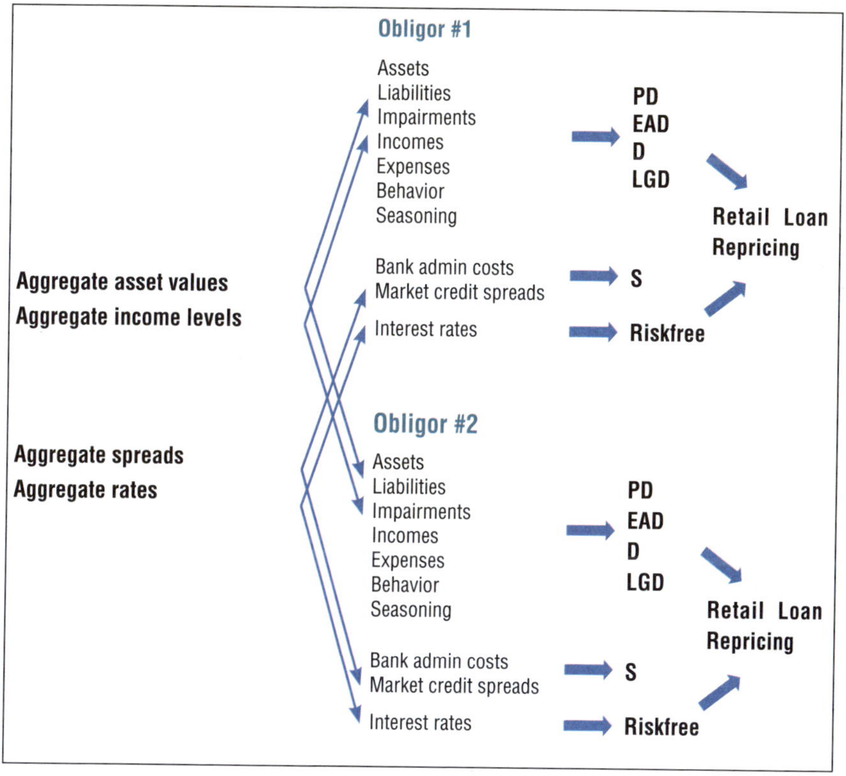

FIGURE 3.3 Risk Map for Two Different Retail Obligors

Because aggregate asset values and income levels affect both obligors, this generally implies a correlation in their estimated PDs and LGDs. The effect of this particular correlation may be underestimated by models that largely rely on historical information to predict defaults. While banks regularly measure market risk in the banking book through aggregate spreads and rates—unless the PD and LGD estimates are sensitive to macro risk—their contribution to credit risk is lost. However, the two main disadvantages of market-linked common credit risk drivers are the need to supply a large number of input parameters to the model and slow computation speed due to higher simulation complexity.

Nevertheless, these correlation relationships have evolved as core components of quantitative credit portfolio models, such as CreditMetrics™, as described in section 3.5.

3.2.2 Default Triggers

To address the problems associated with common risk drivers, many banks use a copula-type approach to induce correlations among obligor defaults.

Copulas create a statistical distribution of events, where a statistical distribution describing a specific combination of events has not previously existed. These distributions can take any shape, including the shape of the normal distribution. By taking the statistical distribution of each event, and linking these events together by making some assumptions about dependence among these events, analysts can create models that help them better understand potential future outcomes.

The mathematics of copulas is complex, so the interested reader is referred to additional literature for further study.[6]

However, it should be noted that copula functions have been blamed for mispricing assets in the years preceding the Global Financial Crisis. Because the copula function used the prices of Credit Default Swaps to calculate correlations, it could only look at time periods when those swaps had existed. Since the swaps had only been in existence for about ten years, and during that time house prices were rising rapidly, there were few examples of default correlations. When prices stopped rising, the number of correlations increased considerably.

EXAMPLE

If a bank owned the third bond to default in a pool of six bonds—a kind of simple collateralized debt obligation (CDO)—it might consider that the risk of default on that third bond would be very low as long as the defaults are uncorrelated. However, it might transpire that the risk of the third bond defaulting is not much different than the risk of the first bond defaulting.

6 See for example "On Default Correlation: A Copula Function Approach" by David X. Li of The RiskMetrics Group, April 2000, available on www.defaultrisk.com and "Copula Modeling: An Introduction for Practitioners" by Priven K. Trivedi and David M. Zimmer, available on www.nowpublishers.com.

Therefore, CDOs are prone to mispricing caused by potentially inaccurate assumptions about risks, particularly correlation risk.

One important advantage of the copula approach is that it can induce correlations in the incidence of default, even if macro-variable influences are present. To avoid the problems of having to specify a large number of correlation parameters between the random numbers being used to simulate defaults, banks often simplify the process using constant correlation rules. Doing so builds on the assumption that a homogeneous group of obligors have largely similar exposures to risks. Two common rules follow this assumption:

1. Assume every obligor has the same correlation to every other obligor
2. Group the obligors by creditor class: assume a high constant correlation within a class, and a low correlation outside the class

Obviously these simplified correlations cannot fully reflect reality but given the alternatives of either a large number of parameters or no correlations at all, they are a good compromise. Furthermore, some banks use observed CDO prices to determine implied correlation estimates.

3.3 Portfolio Measures of Credit Risk

Banks are most interested in determining four types of measures for portfolio credit risk.

- Expected loss (EL) is the aggregate average loss for the credit portfolio and its sub-portfolios. The expected loss is given by the EAD and PD.
- Unexpected loss (UL) is the maximum loss, defined in a probabilistic sense.
- Credit VaR (CVaR) is the difference between EL and UL.
- Factor sensitivities show how the credit portfolio responds to macroeconomic changes.

This information may also be used to estimate the economic capital of the bank, which acts as a capital buffer to guard against unexpected credit losses. Economic capital is estimated at a very high statistical confidence level, so that it is unlikely that such a level of losses would occur.

The first three of these portfolio credit measures are illustrated in the following chart.

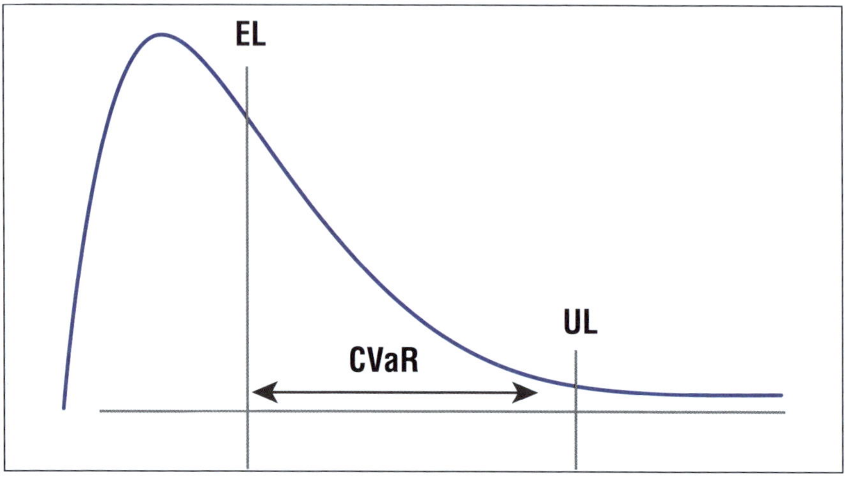

FIGURE 3.4 Distribution of Portfolio Credit Losses

The distribution is plotted in the negative range to indicate losses. The expected loss is the average of the distribution. The unexpected loss is set according to the desired percentile. CVaR, the difference between EL and UL, is expressed as a positive number.

An important point that is often overlooked needs to be emphasized here. Typically, when quantifying market risk, returns on financial assets are assumed to be distributed symmetrically: the likelihood of losses is generally believed to be close to the likelihood of gains. These likelihoods are often modeled using a normal Gaussian distribution or "bell curve" or other symmetrical distributions that may also incorporate salient statistical features of returns on financial assets. However, when looking at the distributions of portfolio credit risk, the shape of the distribution is asymmetric since there is little potential for upside return beyond the terms of the loan obligation, but there is potential for loss caused by default.

Credit portfolios can be aggregated in two ways. One method requires simplifying the individual credit risk exposures so they can be combined analytically into a simplified expression of portfolio risk: this is similar to mapping the risks to common risk factors. A second method requires a simulation of all the underlying macro risk factors, correlated defaults using copulas, and idiosyncratic risks associated with each obligor. The benefits and costs of each method are obvious. The first is prone to model error but is computationally quick. The second is prone to parameter error, and can be slow to compute given the greater simulation complexity. Banks usually draw some kind of compromise between these two extreme methods in order to determine their overall credit portfolio risk.

3.4 Managing the Risk of the Credit Portfolio

Once a bank has understood its credit risk portfolio, it must then decide if and how to manage it. Some possible issues a bank should consider include:

1. *Is the bank taking too much credit risk?*
   A convenient approach to quantify the bank's credit risk exposure is to assess its aggregate EAD at various time points and at various statistical confidence levels. If the level of EAD exceeds the level set by the bank, either because there is insufficient capital to support the actual credit exposures or because the level is not acceptable from a safety and soundness perspective, the risk should be reduced.

   If the EAD cannot be computed, a shortcut is to look at the internal credit rating distribution of the bank. From a senior loan officer, management, or board perspective, aggregate changes in the loan-grade distribution reveal the trend driving the credit risk exposures of the bank. This assumes that there is a common credit risk metric and that the underwriting criteria remain consistent over time and the differences remain solid.

2. *How will this loan add to or subtract from the risk of the existing portfolio?*
   Consider that a bank can lend USD 100 to either Borrower A or Borrower B. Each borrower has a certain amount of risk, although B is riskier. Similarly, each provides a spread over LIBOR (London interbank offered rate) and because of its higher risk, the spread for B is higher. If the bank lends only to A and A defaults, the bank assumes the same loss as if B defaults. If the bank holds just B, the same default situation exists except that the bank will have enjoyed a higher return before default.

   However, if the bank decides to lend to both A and B, then the portfolio can be described as diversified. The bank has shared the likelihood of a negative outcome between these two assets. A core assumption here is that the default of A and B is not fully correlated, so that even if A were to default, it is not certain that B will default, or that

B's default is unlikely to coincide with A's default. It is now important to determine how much benefit such a situation can provide. If the two assets are highly correlated and their asset values move together, then there is no great benefit and the return is simply the weighted average.

If A and B are correlated such that when an action of A has an equal and opposite reaction from B, perfect negative correlation, then there is no additional risk by adding B to the portfolio, and the additional return is a bonus assuming that the holdings are significant. Alternatively, there are diversification benefits to be gained, even if the exposure to B is small.

3. *Is the return from taking credit risk sufficiently high to justify the bank's exposure to the credit?*
The more the bank diversifies its portfolio, the less risky it will be. In debt management, the value of any loan exposure is not expected to substantially appreciate in the same way that an equity investment can. In debt management, the search is not to find the big winners but rather to minimize the effect of any defaults. Moreover, risk-based loan pricing, where internal ratings and loan loss experience drive the pricing grid, helps answer the question.

4. *If this risk is eliminated, can the bank earn a higher return by deploying the capital elsewhere?*
One objective for the risk manager today is to reach what has been called the "efficient frontier." The efficient frontier is a concept developed for investment portfolio management and describes the curve where the ratio between risk and reward is fully optimized.

5. *Will the value of the loan remain stable through to maturity?*
For most credit products, it is relatively easy to find a definition of the market value of a loan: it is the price the loan can be bought or sold for in an open market. Growth in the secondary market for traded loans is providing greater transparency of this information, as previously loan sales were handled privately.

The price of a loan is the combination of all fees and spreads that should compensate the lender for default risk. It is important to remember that default risk cannot be hedged away. It will always exist for the holder of the credit, or for the person that has provided insurance against the default or credit event.

6. *Are there particular areas in the credit portfolio where the bank lacks the risk appetite, expertise, or resources to hold a significant position?* As an integral part of risk governance, managers and credit officers must assess their institution's level of risk appetite when managing their aggregate credit exposures. The lack of risk appetite, the bank's unwillingness to enter a certain segment of the lending spectrum, implies that the bank is neither willing nor otherwise able to accept the risk-return trade-off offered by that particular segment. It is this risk appetite that drives the decision not to enter or to actually exit a particular segment, and these decisions often reflect the credit risk infrastructure of the institution. Typically, the better diversified the bank is from a business perspective, the greater its inherent capacity to effectively operate across various credit segments.

7. *Is there a concentration of portfolio risks due to a large direct or indirect exposure to similar risks and risk factors?* The risks of credit concentration became very evident during the global financial crisis of 2007-2009 after banks had invested heavily in risky mortgages that were underwritten in highly segmented geographical areas.

   A bank has a small number of ways it can manage its credit portfolio. Some elements of the portfolio, such as bonds and marketable securities could simply be sold directly. Other parts of the portfolio can be converted to saleable securities through the process of securitization. Finally, a bank can use credit derivatives to selectively or collectively eliminate credit risks to the portfolio.

The following sections discuss securitization and credit derivatives as risk management tools.

3.4.1 Securitization

Some loans are not sufficiently standardized to be marketed and sold directly, such as credit card loans (a form of revolving credit). Credit card receivables are short term in nature, are not guaranteed by the government, and are not secured by any asset, making them much riskier than mortgage loans from a credit perspective. Banks would find it difficult to sell credit card loans in the same way they sell mortgage loans. However, by standardizing credit card receivables and pooling them into specially created investment vehicles, banks have been able to off-load some of their credit exposures by offering investors the opportunity to buy pools of assets. By pooling residential and commercial mortgages and credit card and other types of receivables in a form that satisfies different risk profiles, banks created specialized and structured securities called Collateralized Mortgage Obligations (CMOs) or CDOs that offered investors premiums that normally arise from a mixture of credit and interest rate risk.

For this reason, banks will often structure asset-backed securities: loans that are backed by assets. In the case of credit card receivables, rather than selling all the credit risk that goes with the receivables, the bank divides the credit card repayments into low-default-risk and high-default-risk cash streams. Each of these streams is called a tranche, meaning a slice or portion. The low-risk stream of cash, known as the senior tranche, would typically be assigned a high credit rating by a rating agency, and would then be sold to investors. This process produces cash for the bank to originate new loans, and eliminates much of the interest rate risk and some of the credit risk of the credit card receivables. However, because the bank is left with the high-risk component of the credit card debt known as the equity tranche, it has not fully eliminated the risk.

EXAMPLE

A bank historically experienced defaults on credit card loans ranging from 0.5% per month to 1% per month. It divides a credit card receivable portfolio on a monthly basis as follows:

- The first 98% of scheduled receivables received in a given month is paid to investors in the senior tranche.
- The last 2% of scheduled receivables is paid to bank, if received, and used to cover costs and losses arising in the future.

The risk of default affecting the first 98% of the receivables pool is small (the monthly default rate would have to exceed 2%) and the senior tranche is given an AA rating. The bank receives a payment that is small and can be highly volatile due to variability in credit losses.

In this example, if the bank could find a buyer for the residual risk of the securitization, it could completely eliminate all of its interest rate risk and credit risk.

3.4.2 Strategic Considerations

As noted in Chapter 2, a substantial proportion of consumer debt has been securitized. There are three reasons securitization is so popular for banks:

- It can be a profit center for the bank
- It generates cash for additional debt origination
- It releases risk and regulatory capital for redeployment (e.g., underwriting of new debt)

Profit center
If the valuation of the structured cash flows exceeds the cost of funding the debt, securitization can be a profit center for the bank. For example, due to structural reasons, portfolio management goals, risk management, or tax issues, debt buyers may pay a premium for a particular tranche of a securitization. In the case of complex securitizations, it is also possible that buyers may misprice the tranches.

Cash efficiency
In the absence of a complete risk transfer, a bank nevertheless increases its cash efficiency by selling off the low-risk portions of the risk. This increases the risk of the residual risk, but it also increases ROE for the bank because of the cash generated by the risk transfer and the overall reduction of the bank's exposure to the risk. Selling the senior tranche, the least risky cash flows in the securitization transaction, is similar to taking a leveraged position in the asset. Although similar, it is not identical, because some risk could still be passed through to the senior tranche if the more junior tranches provide insufficient capital support.

Risk and regulatory capital efficiency
If the credit risk is completely transferred from the bank to the outside investors without recourse, then the bank earns an arbitrage profit. In so doing, it is able to pay off tranche claims in full from the collection proceeds and keep the residual. Also, by completely transferring risk, the securitized asset goes off the bank's balance sheet and is thus no longer included in calculations of economic or regulatory capital, allowing the bank to re-use that capital.

3.4.3 Credit Derivatives

In the 1990s, credit risk management took a leap forward with the development of credit derivatives. The growth of these instruments has arguably been one of the most important developments in credit risk management in recent times. Today there is no doubt that they have improved the liquidity and transferability of credit risk and made pricing more transparent.

While securitization is used to sell credit-linked assets, including some if not all of the credit risk associated with them, credit derivatives are used to transfer the risk on credit that the bank continues to hold in its banking book. The most important credit derivative is the credit default swap (CDS). In a CDS transaction, the buyer of credit protection pays a periodic premium to the seller of protection in exchange for a lump-sum payment in the event of default of the reference entity. A CDS resembles a credit insurance contract, but because it is a derivative, it receives different legal, accounting, and tax treatment.

Figure 3.5 illustrates a sample transaction where the protection buyer pays 50 basis points per year (bppa) of the par bond amount, in exchange for a contingent payment (dotted line) equal to par minus the recovery value of the bond. If the protection buyer owns the bond, the addition of a CDS converts the bond into a risk-free position (except for the counterparty risk of the protection seller).

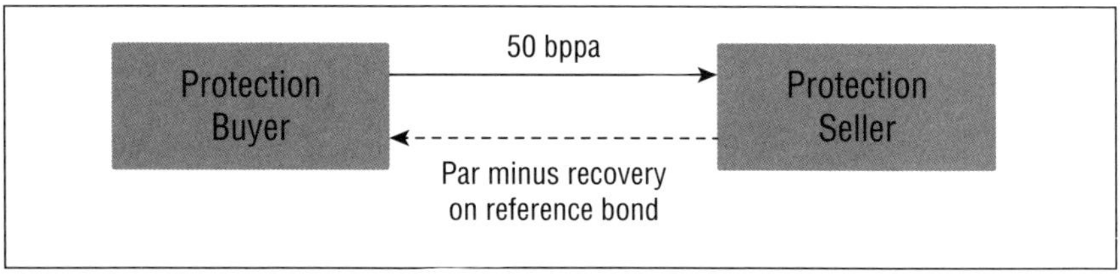

FIGURE 3.5: Sample Credit Derivative Transaction

There are many types of CDS products. Common variations include the substitution of a fixed payment for the par minus recovery payment, and changes in the definition of default. Historically, some of the key risks in credit derivatives have been documentation risk, the definition of credit events, and establishing whether credit events occurred or not. These risks are being addressed with standardized documentation, increased market transparency, and independent services designed to resolve uncertainty and disputes.

Banks can use CDS to move credit risk off their balance sheet if they buy protection from others, or keep it on the balance sheet while transferring credit risk from the banking book to the trading book.

3.4.4 Risks in CDS

The pricing of CDS can be inferred from the pricing of bonds using the following relationship:

$$Risky\ Bond + CDS = Risk\text{-}free\ bond$$

Therefore, pricing is a function of perceived probability of default (PD), loss given default (LGD), and market spreads (S). This pricing relationship is similar to the pricing relationship defined in Chapter 2 with respect to loan pricing. The difference is that because the writer of the CDS is itself vulnerable to default, the relationship is not foolproof.

For the speculative buyer of protection or for the seller of protection, CDS mark-to-market concerns were paramount in 2008. Even without the default of a reference entity (notably Lehman Brothers), repricing of the CDS due to changes in PD, LGD, and S assessments caused massive changes in value. Also, the loss of market liquidity reduced pricing transparency, leading to questionable quotes. The combination of these factors led to huge margin calls which, together with other factors, compromised many financial institutions.

3.4.5 CDS Indices

Whereas a CDS is traded over the counter, a CDS index is a standardized credit security that may offer more liquidity and possibly a narrower bid-ask spread than a single-name derivative contract. It is also likely to be cheaper to hedge a portfolio of bonds with a CDS index than it would be to buy the requisite number of single CDS contracts to achieve a similar hedge.

There are two main providers of CDS indices: S&P and the Markit Group Ltd. S&P produces a number of CDS indices marketed under the name S&P/ISDA, including its S&P/ISDA 100 CDS Index for reference entities of the liquid S&P 100 equity index, S&P/ISDA US High-Yield Index, and S&P/ISDA Eurozone Developed-Nation Sovereign CDS. The Markit Group produces the family of CDX indices which cover North America and emerging market companies and its iTraxx family of indices covering European, Asian, and emerging market companies.

The historical performance of the S&P/ISDA CDS indices is illustrated in the chart below. The S&P/ISDA 100 entities have the lowest spread quotes (in basis points per year), as these companies are mostly investment grade. The investment-grade index shows higher spreads due to inclusion of less creditworthy but still investment-grade companies (e.g., companies with BBB or Baa ratings). The high-yield index shows CDS quotes for companies with ratings below investment grade.

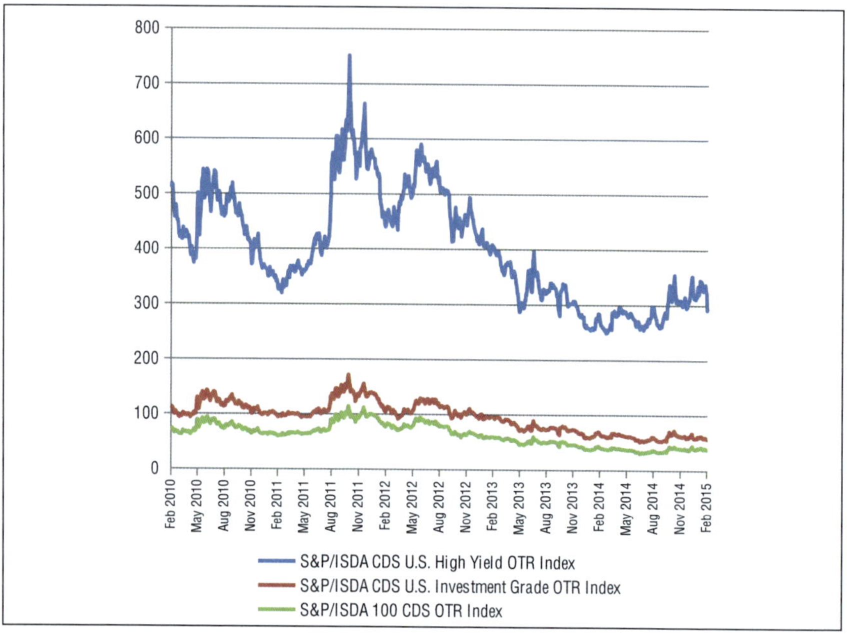

FIGURE 3.6 S&P/ISDA CDS Indices: February 2010–February 2015
Source: www.standardandpoors.com

The data shows the gravity of the European sovereign debt crisis through late 2011 and 2012. (Section 2.5.5 above describes the sovereign debt restructuring of 2012.)

3.4.6 Collateral

Collateral is used by a bank to safeguard its capital and acts as insurance in case the borrower cannot repay its loan. In the event of default, the bank has the option of accepting the collateral as full or partial repayment of the loan's principal, accrued interest, fees and costs, and expenses. As such, collateral plays a major role in a bank's credit risk management as it mitigates or eliminates the effect of the borrower's default.

Collateral has many forms and can be financial or non-financial collateral. Cash is the most obvious and most secure form of collateral as it is the most liquid.

Financial collateral typically consists of:

- Cash, Certificates of Deposit (CDs), and other deposits
- Gold
- Publicly rated bonds issued by sovereign banks and other entities, subject to minimum rating grades
- Unrated bonds issued and traded on a recognized exchange
- Equities and convertible bonds included in a main market index, or otherwise traded or tradable
- Mutual fund shares and similar unit investment vehicles, subject to daily quotes being available

Non-financial collateral typically consists of:

- Real estate (developed or undeveloped, including timberland and mineral rights)
- Receivables (commercial debts owed to a company)
- Machinery, equipment, patents, and copyrights
- Stake in privately held business

Typically, banks lend up to 100% against cash collateral but cash is not widely used as a primary collateral. Instead, borrowers often pledge various assets that they own to provide additional credit support for their borrowing. In their credit policy, banks establish various "haircuts," reductions in the value of the collateral, that determine how much credit the collateral can support. For instance, a 10% haircut means that a USD 1,000 asset can provide collateral support up to USD 900. Note that haircuts and loan-to-value ratios are related: a 10% haircut equals a 90% loan-to-value ratio. Because collateral can be subject to fluctuations in value, the haircut applied depends on factors such as the liquidity, revaluation frequency, and quality of the collateral.

Collateral Type	Haircut	Typical LTV range
Government bonds	up to 10%	More than 90%
Securities (stocks, bonds)	at least 25%	75% or less
Real estate	at least 20%	80% or less
Receivables	at least 25%	75% or less
Inventory	at least 25%	25 – 75%
Machinery	at least 25%	25 – 75%

FIGURE 3.7 Collateral type, Haircut, and Typical LTV Range

There are numerous practical problems when accepting collateral to support lending. The first relates to legal requirements: the borrower's pledging of the collateral as a non-primary repayment source has to be legally enforceable. This often means that the collateral should be unencumbered, and that the borrower should have ownershipof the collateral or the explicit right to dispose of the collateral in a manner that allows pledging.

The second problem relates to the relationship between the collateral and the loan. From a credit risk management perspective, the credit quality of the borrower, and the value of the collateral should be unrelated, e.g., an oil refinery should not use its equity stake in another refinery as collateral for a loan. Limiting this relationship achieves the objective of collateral: securing a secondary source of repayment in case the primary source of repayment becomes inadequate due to the borrower's inability or unwillingness to pay. Avoiding this correlation is easier said than done, particularly in SME lending or lending to privately held companies. In SME collateral requests, many banks use the principals' ownership stake in the corporation as the primary collateral against the loan. If the loan is not paid back on time, the ownership reverts to the bank, which then becomes the owner of the SME.

The third relates to marketability. Banks prefer liquid assets as collateral because these assets can be easily disposed of in case the bank becomes the owner of the collateral. That is why publicly traded financial assets generally have a very low haircut. Illiquid or less liquid collateral, such as real estate and stakes in privately held companies, may not be easy to dispose. When easy disposition is limited, many banks seek to manage the underlying asset until it can be sold.

3.5 An Overview of Credit Portfolio Management Models

Banks use various portfolio credit models to quantify their credit risk exposures by modeling factors that impact the credit risk of an asset, and by extension, the value of the credit portfolio and the value of the bank. Credit portfolio models are complex because they model the likelihood and the potential value effect of a credit event, such as:

- Non-payment or bankruptcy (default risk)
- Downgrade in internal or external credit ratings (migration risk)
- Changing price of credit without a change in the underlying credit rating (spread risk)
- Changes in the value of collateral and recoverability (recovery risk)

Changes in default risk, migration risk, spread risk, and recovery risk all impact the value of the exposure, and by extension the price of the exposure and the mark-to-market value of the exposures, that is recorded on the books of the bank.

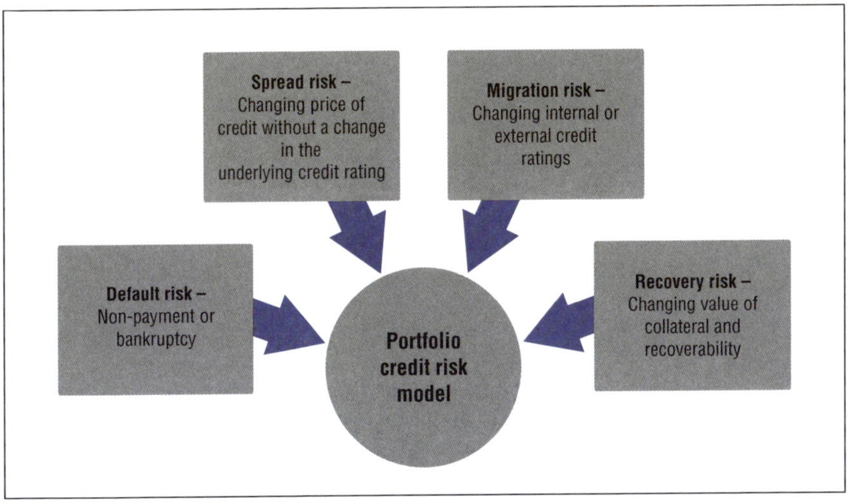

FIGURE 3.8 Portfolio Credit Risk Model

Some banks develop their own proprietary models, and these have the advantage of customization to allow for more complex instruments or portfolios, the inclusion of region-specific correlation factors, and comprehensive stress-testing scenarios. However, given the complexity of such models and therefore the need for specialized expertise, most banks rely on one of a number of commercially available models which include:

- CreditMetrics™ was originally devised by JPMorgan's Risk Management Research division, which later became the RiskMetrics Group. CreditMetrics™ includes a number of frameworks such as the Hull-White pricing framework which allows user-estimated recovery rates and collateral in default and non-default and thereby can be used to price a range of credit asset types such as commitments, CDS's, letters of credit, etc.
- Kamakura Risk Manager, from Kamakura Corporation. This is a multiple-models risk management system using a variety of structural and reduced-form methodologies to model default probabilities for corporates, non-public firms, and sovereigns including the simulation of macroeconomic factors.
- Moody's Analytics, part of Moody's Corporation. This produces a suite of credit portfolio models including RiskCalc™, which is a financial-ratio-based model for deriving PDs for private companies. Other models are CreditEdge, an enhanced Merton model for public companies, and Moody's Portfolio Analyzer, a stress-testing and capital allocation model designed specifically for use in auto loan, residential mortgages, and auto ABS and RMBS portfolios.
- CreditPortfolioView™, from McKinsey. This models the link between a transition probability and an index of macroeconomic activity.

Using sophisticated mathematical techniques, these models seek to predict the likelihood that a simple car loan goes bad, as well as the likelihood that thousands of car loans default on the same day as a major car manufacturer defaults on one of its loans. These models are extremely complex, and in their quest to quantify hard-to-measure losses at very high levels of statistical confidence, they rely on simplifying modeling assumptions. Nevertheless, information from these models assists many banks worldwide to establish credit limits across geographies, industries, and assets classes.

Types of credit portfolio risk models

Whether a credit portfolio model is commercially available or has been internally developed, it can be classified according to a number of criteria. These typically include: how exposures are aggregated, how risks are quantified, how the macroeconomic environment impacts the model, and how default correlations are modeled.

Transaction-driven and global models

Portfolio credit risk models can be transaction-driven or global models. In a transaction-driven or bottom-up model, each credit exposure is modeled separately and then aggregated first at a homogenous sub-portfolio level, and then at increasingly heterogeneous levels before it is aggregated at the global portfolio level. On the other hand, global or top-down models determine factors that drive the performance of the entire global portfolio comprised of homogenous sub-portfolios. Here the individual transaction and exposure is less important.

For corporate loan exposures, transaction-driven models are more appropriate because the credit risk estimates are better at comprehensively reflecting the overall risk of individual financial performance factors impacting the specific exposure. For homogenous retail exposures, global models work better due to the reduced complexity of modeling a few global economic factors that determine the overall value of the exposure.

Default models and credit-value models

Although credit portfolio models seek to predict the expected value of the exposure, some models focus on changes in the credit quality of individual loans as well as the risk of defaults. Others focus solely on assessing the risk of default and how changes in the estimated default risk can or should impact the value of the individual exposure and by extension, and through aggregation, the collective value of all exposures.

For credit-value models, changes in economic, financial, and other factors that can impact credit spreads, ratings changes, and fluctuations in collateral values are relevant, but they are not relevant to default models whose sole focus is changes in the risk of default.

There are also models that jointly consider default risk, credit risk, spread risk, migration risk, and recovery risk.

Macroeconomic effects
Most credit portfolio models incorporate the effects of changing macroeconomic variables such as growth, interest rates, default rates, etc., in their computation of credit risks. These models typically incorporate empirical evidence that during economic expansion default rates decline and credit migration is generally positive, accompanied by a narrowing of credit spreads. The inverse, economic contraction, presages both increased incidence of defaults, downward credit rating migration, and widening credit spreads.

Other models are more focused on borrower-specific changes in credit quality, where macroeconomic factors may not be considered explicitly, but only through specific modeling, i.e., stress testing.

Default-probability modeling
Whether models focus on predicting default or predicting value changes, how the impact of defaults is modeled is highly relevant. As defaults tend to correlate, some models establish joint default probabilities using structural models, while others use background factors.

3.5.1 The Black Box

Credit portfolio models are calculation-driven models where the value is determined by a series of increasingly complex calculations, which may not always be easily penetrable or transparent for an outsider. In simple terms, such a quantitative black-box model seeks to quantify the risks of individual exposures using statistical modeling and analysis. By taking financial, performance, and credit data from different historical sources, credit portfolio models seek to create a large range of various hypothetical values through a combination of statistical or mathematical analysis and Monte Carlo simulation. That large range of hypothetical values then creates probability distributions. Various statistical confidence intervals determine the potential value impact on individual exposures over a set time period.

The following graph depicts the components and structure of CreditMetrics™, a commercially available credit risk model.

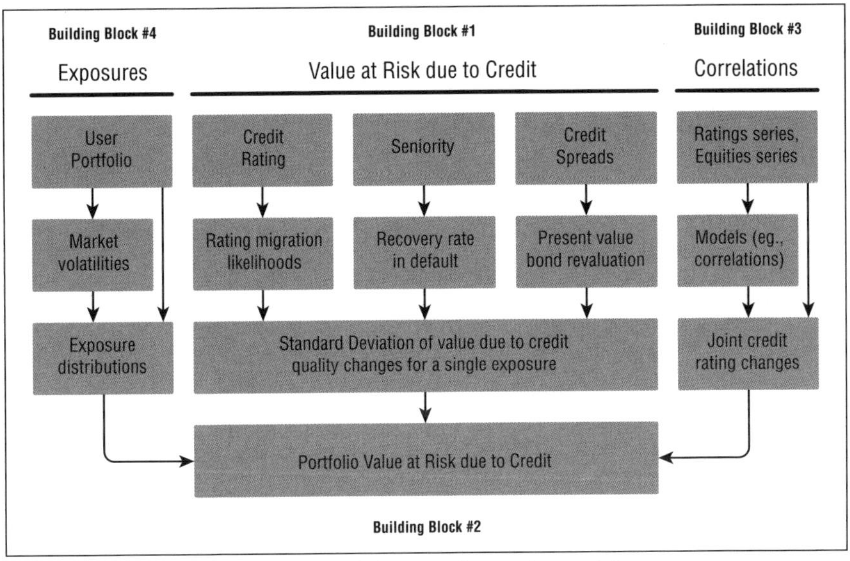

FIGURE 3.9 CreditMetrics Portfolio Credit Risk Model
Source: http://www.riskmetrics.com/publications/techdoc.html .

This particular model consists of four related building blocks. The first building block computes CreditVaR for individual exposures by separately modeling credit migration, recovery risk, and changes in spread. These determine the risk of an individual exposure, which is then aggregated across the various portfolios (which is the second building block). The process is supported by modeling correlations and assessing the risk contribution of individual exposures.

Unlike market-risk models, where time horizon is computed on a daily basis, these credit risk models estimate the collective impact of credit risk—migration, spread, default, and recovery—over a longer time period. The Basel Accords require capital requirements for credit risk of estimated expected and unexpected losses over a one-year horizon, so most credit models predict the expected and unexpected losses over a one-year period. Moreover, each model may have a core risk driver. For instance, macroeconomic factors impact default risk and credit spreads, interest rates, and attributes of each transaction. The value of the credit portfolio is also affected by the structure and composition of the portfolio. For instance, a portfolio of fixed-rate loans would have a weaker link between default risk and interest rates than a floating-rate portfolio.

The one-year time period is not only a result of regulatory requirements. It also reflects practical considerations. While exchange and interest rates as well as equity and commodity prices change on a daily basis, default and credit rating changes are less regular, and are more likely to occur over a one-year horizon than a one-day horizon. In addition, access to secondary markets and the market liquidity of credit assets and financial market instruments is different: selling a loan to another bank or syndicating a loan exposure takes longer than selling bonds on the financial markets. These differences in liquidity can become particularly significant during times of market stress when loan pricing transparency is limited and liquidity is elusive. Finally, the maturity of credit products may be difficult to compute, particularly for contingent credit products such as loan commitments or letters of credit.

While expected losses are covered through loan loss provisions and allowance for loan losses, unexpected losses should be covered through capital provisions. Both expected and unexpected loss need to be priced into a loan, but while the expected loss compensates the bank for the losses it should reasonably expect on various credit exposures, the unexpected losses must be priced to provide adequately risk-adjusted return to shareholders.

3.5.2 Comparing Credit Risk Models

The four main credit risk models are different; Figure 3.10 summarizes the salient features of each.

Model	CreditMetrics™	RiskFrontier™	Kamakura Risk Manager™	CreditPortfolioView™
Source	RiskMetrics (JPMorgan)	Moody's Analytics	Kamakura Corporation	McKinsey
Risk Focus	Migration, default, recovery	Migration, default, recovery	Migration, default, recovery	Migration, default, recovery
Transaction/ Global	Transaction	Transaction	Transaction	Global
Macroeffects	Explicitly considers	May consider	Explicitly considers	May consider
Core Risk Driver	Asset value	Asset value	Interest rates	Macro factors

FIGURE 3.10 Overview of Commercially Available Credit Risk Models

3.5.3 Problems with Credit Portfolio Models

Credit portfolio models have gained substantial acceptance in banks but they have some shortcomings. A frequent criticism comes from the inability to backtest the model's results. While Market VaR models can be and are backtested, these credit portfolio models—which mimic the Market VaR methodology—cannot be backtested to ensure that their predictive performance is congruent with historical records.

Further, these credit portfolio models may treat EAD or RR as readily known factors that may not need to be modeled separately within the system. However, there may be common factors that jointly impact both of these variables. For instance in the case of OTC derivatives, default may be caused by the declining value of exposures, which increases the EAD. At the same time, and due to declining asset values, a counterparty may opt for a strategic default, which could reduce the recoverable value.

3.5.4 Uses of Credit Portfolio Models

Apart from estimating regulatory capital requirements, the chief uses of these models include loan pricing, risk-adjusted performance measurement, maximizing the risk-return trade-off of the portfolio, and establishing credit limits. In addition to these uses, the models yield results that can be used to implement hedging credit exposures.

Loan pricing

Banks often use their own credit ratings on clients to price their loans. Credit portfolio models offer a broader analytical perspective because they allow a bank to consider more factors that may impact the risk and return on the loan, including the diversification benefits derived from individual loans. Moreover, as credit portfolio models can quantify unexpected losses, the cost of funding individual credits can consider the economic cost of the capital the bank needs to raise in support of the loan.

Risk-adjusted performance measurement

Credit portfolio models offer estimates of expected and unexpected losses as well as performance metrics on the portfolio. This allows the bank to analyze and compare individual exposures separately and collectively to identify performance that considers the inherent risk of the loan.

Maximizing the risk-return trade-off of the portfolio
Credit portfolio models allow the bank to analyze and compare the performance of exposures and loans, both individually and in the aggregate. This allows the bank to identify loans that offer attractive risk and performance metrics, and those loans that may not positively contribute to the overall risk-adjusted performance of the portfolio. By realigning the composition of the portfolio, the risk-return trade-off can be optimized using these models.

Establishing credit limits
By analyzing the risk of various operating units based on the loans that they have generated, the bank can establish risk and operating limits that consider the credit quality of the specific loans that the various business units underwrite. In fact, credit portfolio models can be used to successfully establish internal lending limits for various branches by taking into consideration the performance of loans typically underwritten. Loan limits can be adapted to reflect the risk differences across sectors, industries, and countries or other geographic areas.

3.6 Problem Asset Management

Problem assets are managed in workout units that have extensive experience with lending, dealing with complex credit products, working with various types of borrowers, and working across a range of industrial sectors. Executed well, their efforts can avoid painful losses to a bank. Workout units deal with a wide spectrum of distressed borrowers ranging from those who can pay but choose to default, those who cannot pay as agreed, and those who proactively act to remedy their distressed situation.

An integral part of the process is the assessment of various legal avenues to ensure that the bank maintains a security interest in the assets and collateral underlying the loans. Typically, workout units often actively pursue various legal options for recovery.

The remit of the workout specialist team is to recover as much as possible so as to reduce the overall potential loss to the bank from a default. In the case of retail lending, this can be accompanied by modifying loan terms, extending additional credit, or liquidating the collateral. In business lending, this can be achieved by modifying loan terms, extending additional credit to bridge a difficult situation, recommending business, operational, and strategic changes, or liquidating any collateral by actively soliciting potential buyers. In a default situation, the workout officer may actually end up managing the distressed company until a suitable buyer to the company can be found.

3.6.1 Managing Problem Assets

Before a loan is assigned to a workout specialist, the bank should have identified the borrower's difficulties and re-assigned the borrower's internal rating e.g., from "acceptable" to "substandard" or "doubtful," etc.

As a loan begins to deteriorate, it is essential to gather as much information as possible. Consequently, the workout officer must focus upon the borrower's ability to generate sufficient cash to meet all of its on-going legal and contractual obligations, including those to the bank. Often modifying repayment terms through extending the repayment period or temporarily reducing interest payments can help the borrower to strengthen its ability to generate long-term cash flow and ultimately ensure repayment.

Some lenders assume that obtaining comprehensive and accurate borrower information is the only way to assess a deteriorating situation, but there are reasons why obtaining basic information quickly is often better than delayed comprehensive information:

- Management is sometimes oblivious to any developing problems. Therefore it becomes critical for the workout specialist to convince management of the gravity of the deteriorating situation, and the need to make difficult decisions.
- For many borrowers in the retail and manufacturing sectors, their largest asset is their inventory. This means that inventory may need to be quickly sold in order to generate as much cash flow as possible. However, obsolescence is a problem for many retail borrowers.
- Most borrowers rely on their suppliers. Core suppliers must be contacted in order to discuss how to avoid any slowdown or cessation of raw materials delivery. Often, banks seek to ensure that the business continues to operate by providing financing to its main suppliers and core customers. Systemic problems can easily hit a solid and well-capitalized borrower that is integrated in a supply chain.
- Employees will generally know when there are problems. Employee morale will suffer (an early warning signal of a company's operational problems). Employees may become unmotivated and lose interest in the company. A bank needs to reassure employees that they will continue to be paid in a timely manner.

The workout officer must establish a workout plan aimed at maximizing the likelihood of full recovery. The workout plan should contain the various elements of financial support—modifying loan terms, extending additional credit, etc.—as well as outlining the business, operational, and strategic steps the borrower should take to ensure that ongoing capital support to the troubled borrower can continue.

3.6.2 Asset Management Companies or Bad Banks

In the last several years, the bad bank or aggregator bank solution has emerged as an alternative to managing a bank's troubled or otherwise non-performing assets. Typically, this solution is pursued when a bank has suffered considerable debilitating losses and is required to separate its non-performing assets from its portfolio. In some cases, this is also a regulatory requirement imposed on banks as a condition of continued operations. The separation process involves the creation of an asset management company (AMC). An AMC may or may not be a subsidiary of the bank, and is an efficient solution for banks faced with the legal and technical challenges of a large problem-loan portfolio. The separate entity allows the bank's management to focus on running the bank. By creating such an entity, banks are relieved of the responsibility of dealing with non-performing assets, including regulatory requirements that are typically imposed on non-performing assets.

After the non-performing assets are transferred to the AMC, the assets are restructured and made attractive to potential buyers. To make these assets more marketable, workout specialists may choose to restructure the troubled business by bringing in new management, divesting non-performing business units, or pooling business lines in order to improve the overall viability of the business. This process can be lengthy, but it provides a price support to the assets compared to the alternative: quick resale in a market saturated by other banks seeking to unwind similar non-performing portfolios. This requires the AMC to be both well capitalized and have a long mandate. During the Swedish banking crisis in the early 1990s, the AMCs had a 15-year mandate to unwind and recover the assets. In fact, within five years, these AMCs were dissolved as the loans and troubled assets were repackaged and sold to investors, in some cases for a significant profit.

EXAMPLE

The collapse of the Irish property market starting in late 2008 caused a severe crisis in its banking sector. In a bid to facilitate commercial lending to support economic growth, the Irish government established the National Asset Management Agency (NAMA) to acquire the riskiest loan portfolios, mainly land and development loans, from the books of systemically important financial institutions.

During 2010 and 2011, the agency acquired approximately 12,000 loans issued with 60,000 properties as security from 800 debtors from five financial institutions. The acquisition was funded by equity stakes taken by the government, three private institutions, and the issuance of EUR 30.2 billion in senior debt. By the end of 2014, NAMA had redeemed EUR 16.6 billion of its senior loans, two years ahead of the 50% senior debt redemption target originally set for the end of 2016. The original plan assumed a life of 11 years for NAMA with full repayment of the debt issued by 2020.

3.6.3 Avoiding Bad Loans

There are few ways a bank can reduce the likelihood of increased default in its credit portfolio. Thorough and structured credit analysis is only the first step. Ongoing dialogue between the bank and the borrower is widely seen as the key tool in reducing the likelihood of default. Understanding the borrower's character and the business operating conditions mitigates potential difficulties. Unfortunately, this advice is often overlooked, largely due to the large number of relationships a loan officer has to manage. Bankers should visit their clients on a quarterly basis, but with large portfolios, this is generally impossible to achieve. This violates one of the core tenets of lending: managing the lending relationship by creating an ongoing assessment of needs, discussing facts, and recommending viable solutions.

3.6.4 Estimating Recovery Rates on Problem Assets

Recovering problem assets and creating workout solutions is a trade-off between the actual cost of recovery and the expected value recovered on the problem asset. In prioritizing the decisions in the recovery process, the manager should consider the following factors:

- The accounting value of the problem asset, including any chargeable and accrued fees
- Exposure at default

- The administrative expenses associated with the recovery and workout, separate from the fees related to the actual loan
- The risk-adjusted recovery discount rate, which reflects the market rates between default and recovery
- The duration of the recovery process and the size and direction of any intermittent cash flows

In simple terms, the recovery rate is given as:

$$RR = \{(AV/EAD) \times [(AV - \text{Recovery Expenses})/AV)]\}/(1 + \text{Recovery Discount Rate})^{\text{Duration}}$$

where AV is the Accounting Value of the asset

EXAMPLE

One of Bank D's counterparties defaulted on a USD 20 million trade. One year later USD 5 million was recovered after the bank had spent USD 0.5 million. Using a 10% discount rate to reflect the prevailing market conditions, the recovery rate is 20.45%.

3.7 Credit Risk Reporting: JP Morgan Chase

Credit risk reporting is one of the most critical business processes in a modern bank. There are two categories: internal reporting and external reporting of credit risk exposures. For external reporting, overestimating past, present, and future credit exposures may mislead shareholders, while underestimating them may displease regulators and lead to substantial fines. Internal reporting, on the other hand, allows managers at different levels to analyze and manage credit risk from the portfolio level to the individual-credit-position level.

Common reports are: aggregate credit exposure, credit quality forecasts, concentration levels, and risk profile changes.

Regulatory oversight is discussed in greater detail in Chapter 4, however, it is important to note here that in order to improve market discipline through increased transparency, the Basel III framework has implemented deeper and broader disclosure standards. The objective of these changes is to ensure that market participants have an increased ability to better assess the risks other banks may pose.

December 31, 2013 (In millions)	Credit exposure 2013	Credit exposure 2012	Nonperforming [c][d][e] 2013	Nonperforming [c][d][e] 2012
Loans retained	$ 724,177	$ 726,835	$ 8,317	$ 10,609
Loans held-for-sale	12,230	4,406	26	18
Loans at fair value [a]	2,011	2,555	197	265
Total loans - reported	738,418	733,796	8,540	10,892
Derivative receivables	65,759	74,983	415	239
Receivables from customers and other	26,883	23,761	-	-
Total credit-related assets	831,060	832,540	8,955	11,131
Assets acquired in loan satisfactions				
Real estate owned	NA	NA	710	738
Other	NA	NA	41	37
Total assets acquired in loan satisfactions	NA	NA	751	775
Total assets	831,060	832,540	9,706	11,906
Lending-related commitments	1,031,672	1,027,988	206	355
Total credit portfolio	$1,862,732	$1,860,528	$9,912	$12,261
Credit Portfolio Management derivatives notional.net [b]	(27,996)	(27,447)	(5)	(25)
Liquid securities and other cash collateral held against derivatives	(14,435)	(15,201)	NA	NA
Year ended December 31, (in millions, except ratios)		**2013**		**2012**
Net charge-offs [f]		$ 5,802		$ 9,063
Average retained loans				
Loans - reported		720,152		717,035
Loans - reported, excluding residential real estate PCI loans		663,629		654,454
Net charge-off rates [f]				
Loans - reported		0.81%		1.26%
Loans - reported, excluding PCI		0.87		1.38

(a) During 2013, certain loans that resulted from restructurings that were previously classified as performing were reclassified as nonperforming loans. Prior periods were revised to conform with the current presentation.
(b) Represents the net notional amount of protection purchased and sold through credit derivatives used to manage both performing and nonperforming wholesale credit exposures: these derivatives do not qualify for hedge accounting under U.S. GAAP. Excludes the synthetic credit portfolio. For additional information, see Credit derivatives on pages 137-138 and Note 6 on pages 220-233 of this Annual Report.
(c) Excludes PCI loans. The Firm is recognizing interest income on each pool of PCI loans as they are all performing.
(d) At December 31, 2013 and 2012, nonperforming assets excluded: (1) mortgage loans insured by U.S. government agencies of USD 8.4 billion and USD 10.6 billion, respectively, that are 90 or more days past due; (2) real estate owned insured by U.S. government agencies of USD 2.0 billion and USD 1.6 billion, respectively; and (3) student loans insured by U.S. government agencies under the FFELP of USD 428 million and USD 525 million, respectively, that are 90 or more days past due. These amounts have been excluded from nonaccrual loans based upon the government guarantee. In addition, the Firm's policy is generally to exempt credit card loans from being placed on nonaccrual status as permitted by regulatory guidance issued by the Federal Financial Institutions Examination Council ("FFIEC").
(e) At December 31, 2013 and 2012, total nonaccrual loans represented 1.16% and 1.48%, respectively, of total loans.
(f) Net charge-offs and net charge-off rates for the year ended December 31, 2012, included USD 800 million of incremental charge-offs of Chapter 7 loans. See Consumer Credit Portfolio on pages 120-129 of this Annual Report for further details.

FIGURE 3.11 JP Morgan Chase's Total Credit Portfolio
Source: JP Morgan Chase 2013 Annual Report

In the example above, in 2013, JP Morgan had an aggregate credit portfolio, including derivatives receivables and lending commitments, of almost USD 1.9 trillion.

3.7.1 Wholesale Portfolio

Management of wholesale credit risk exposure is generally accomplished using one or more of the following:

- Loan underwriting and credit approval process
- Loan syndications and participations
- Loan sales and securitizations
- Credit derivatives
- Use of master netting agreements
- Collateral and other risk-reduction techniques

Wholesale credit risk reporting is often broken down by industry, as Figure 3.12 illustrates:

			Noninvestment-grade[e]			Selected metrics			
As of or for the year ended December 31, 2013 (in millions)	Credit exposure[d]	Investment-grade	Non-criticized	Criticized performing	Criticized non-performing	30 days or more past due and accruing loans	Net charge-offs/ (recoveries)	Credit derivative hedges[f]	Liquid securities & other cash collateral held against derivative receivables
Top 25 industries[a]									
Real Estate	$ 87,102	$ 62,964	$ 21,505	$ 2,286	$ 347	$ 178	$ 6	$ (66)	$ (125)
Bank & Finance Cos	66,881	56,675	9,707	431	68	14	(22)	(2,692)	(6,227)
Oil & Gas	46,934	34,708	11,779	436	11	34	13	(227)	(67)
Healthcare	45,910	37,635	7,952	317	6	49	3	(198)	(195)
State & Municipal Govt[b]	35,666	34,563	826	157	120	40	1	(161)	(144)
Consumer Products	34,145	21,100	12,505	537	3	4	11	(149)	(1)
Asset Managers	33,506	26,991	6,477	38	-	217	(7)	(5)	(3,191)
Utilities	28,938	25,521	3,045	411	6	2	28	(445)	(306)
Retail & Consumer Services	25,068	16,101	8,453	492	22	6	-	(91)	-
Technology	21,403	13,787	6,771	825	20	-	-	(512)	-
Central Govt	21,049	20,633	345	71	-	-	-	(10,088)	(1,541)
Machinery & Equipment Mfg	19,078	11,154	7,549	368	7	20	(18)	(257)	(8)
Metals/Mining	17,434	9,266	7,508	594	66	1	16	(621)	(36)
Business Services	14,601	7,838	6,447	286	30	9	10	(10)	(2)
Transportation	13,975	9,683	4,165	100	27	10	8	(68)	-
Telecom Services	13,906	9,130	4,284	482	10	-	7	(272)	(8)
Media	13,858	7,783	5,658	315	102	6	36	(26)	(5)
Insurance	13,761	10,681	2,757	84	239	-	(2)	(98)	(1,935)
Building Materials/ Construction	12,901	5,701	6,354	839	7	15	3	(132)	-
Automotive	12,532	7,881	4,490	159	2	3	(3)	(472)	-
Chemicals/Plastics	10,637	7,189	3,211	222	15	-	-	(13)	(83)
Securities Firms & Exchanges	10,035	7,781	2,233	14	7	1	(68)	(4,169)	(175)
Agriculture/Paper Mfg	7,387	4,238	3,064	82	3	31	-	(4)	(4)
Aerospace/Defense	6,873	5,447	1,426	-	-	-	-	(142)	(1)
Leisure	5,331	2,950	1,797	495	89	5	-	(10)	(14)
All other[c]	201,298	180,460	19,911	692	235	1,249	(6)	(7,068)	(367)
Subtotal	$ 820,254	$ 637,860	$ 170,219	$ 10,733	$ 1,442	$ 1,894	$ 16	$ (27,996)	$ (14,435)
Loans held-for-sale and loans at fair value	13,301								
Receivables from customers and other	26,744								
Total	$ 860,299								

FIGURE 3.12 JP Morgan Chase's Wholesale Credit Portfolio
Source: JP Morgan Chase 2013 Annual Report

Figure 3.12 shows that lending to the real estate industry formed the largest segment of wholesale lending for JP Morgan Chase in 2013, with over 10% of credit exposure in this portfolio.

A further aspect of wholesale portfolio credit risk is related to derivatives. When the market price of a derivative contract changes and a bank, as a result, becomes a net creditor to its counterparties, the credit risk in the portfolio increases.

Aggregate Notional Principal Amounts (NPAs) are often not very helpful to report. It is more useful to know the Mark-to-Market (M-t-M) value of a position or a portfolio, as this helps the risk manager to understand the credit risk in the derivatives portfolio in credit- or loan-equivalent terms. A loan valued at USD 5 million has approximately the same value as a derivative with a USD 5 million M-t-M value at that point in time.

Figure 3.13 shows JPMorgan Chase's exposure profile calculated using derivative risk equivalent (DRE) and average exposure (AVG).

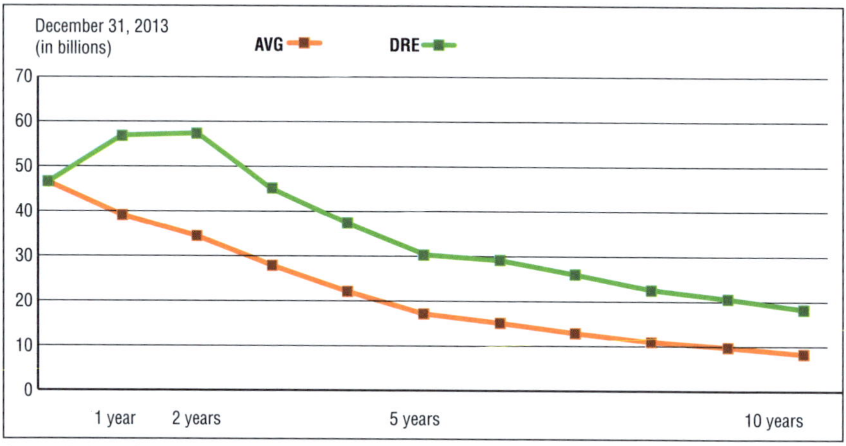

Source: JP Morgan Chase 2013 Annual Report

FIGURE 3.13 Exposure Profile of Derivatives Measures

Derivatives exposures can also be reported on a time basis, using either maturity or duration as the yardstick, as well as on a counterparty-credit risk (CCR) basis, using public ratings.

Rating Equivalent	**2013**		**2012**	
December 31, (in millions, except ratios)	**Exposure net of all collateral**	**% of exposure net of all collateral**	**Exposure net of all collateral**	**% of exposure net of all collateral**
AAA/Aaa to AA-/Aa3	$ 12,453	24%	$ 19,964	34%
A+/A1 to A-/A3	17,243	34	12,039	20
BBB+/Baa1 to BBB-/Baa3	14,981	29	18,066	30
BB+/Ba1 to B-/B3	5,820	11	8,434	14
CCC+/Caa1 and below	827	2	1,279	2
Total	$ 51,324	100%	$ 59,782	100%

FIGURE 3.14 Ratings Profile of JPMorgan's Derivative Receivables
Source: JP Morgan Chase 2013 Annual Report

3.7.2 Retail Portfolio

Consumer credit exposures are typically concentrated in the following areas:

- Residential real estate loans
- Credit card loans
- Auto loans
- Business banking loans
- Student loans

As of or for the year ended December 31, (in millions, except ratios)	Credit Exposure		Nonaccrual Loans [f] [g]		Net Charge-offs [h] [i]		Average Annual Net Charge-off Rate [h] [i] [j]	
	2013	2012	2013	2012	2013	2012	2013	2012
Consumer, excluding credit card								
Loans, excluding PCI loans and loans held-for sale								
Home equity - senior lien	$ 17,113	$ 19,385	$ 932	$ 931	$ 132	$ 279	0.72	1.33
Home equity - junior lien	40,750	48,000	1,876	2,277	834	2,106	1.90	4.07
Prime mortgage, including option ARMs	87,162	7,626	2,666	3,445	59	487	0.07	0.64
Subprime mortgage	7,104	8,255	1,390	1,807	90	486	1.17	5.43
Auto [a]	52,757	49,913	161	163	158	188	0.31	0.39
Business banking	18,951	18,883	385	481	337	411	1.81	2.27
Student and other	11,557	12,191	86	70	297	340	2.51	2.58
Total loans, excluding PCI loans and loans held-for-sale	235,394	232,883	7,496	9,174	1,907	4,297	0.82	1.81
Loans - PCI								
Home equity	18,927	20,971	NA	NA	NA	NA	NA	NA
Prime mortgage	12,038	13,674	NA	NA	NA	NA	NA	NA
Subprime mortgage	4,175	4,626	NA	NA	NA	NA	NA	NA
Option ARMs	17,915	20,466	NA	NA	NA	NA	NA	NA
Total loans - PCI	53,055	59,737	NA	NA	NA	NA	NA	NA
Total loans - retained	288,449	292,620	7,496	9,174	1,907	4,297	0.66	1.43
Loans held-for-sale [b]	614	-	-	-	-	-	-	-
Total consumer, excluding credit card loans	289,063	292,620	7,496	9,174	1,907	4,297	0.66	1.43
Lending-related commitments								
Home equity - senior lien [c]	13,158	15,180						
Home equity - junior lien [c]	17,837	21,796						
Prime mortgage	4,817	4,107						
Subprime mortgage	-	-						
Auto	8,309	7,185						
Business banking	11,251	11,092						
Student and other	685	796						
Total lending-related commitments	56,057	60,156						
Receivables from customers [d]	139	113						
Total consumer exposure, excluding credit card	345,259	352,889						
Credit Card								
Loans retained [e]	127,465	127,993	-	1	3,879	4,944	3.14	3.95
Loans held-for-sale	326	-	-	-	-	-	-	-
Total credit card loans	127,791	127,993	-	1	3,879	4,944	3.14	3.95
Lending-related commitments [c]	529,383	533,018						
Total credit card exposure	657,174	661,011						
Total consumer credit portfolio	$ 1,002,433	$ 1,013,900	$ 7,496	$ 9,175	$ 5,786	$ 9,241	1.4%	2.17%
Memo: total consumer credit portfolio, excluding PCI	$ 949,378	$ 954,163	$ 7,496	$ 9,175	$ 5,786	$ 9,241	1.62%	2.55%

(a) At December 31, 2013 and 2012, excluded operating lease-related assets of USD 5.5 billion and USD 4.7 billion, respectively.
(b) Represents prime mortgage loans held-for-sale.
(c) Credit card and home equity lending-related commitments represent the total available lines of credit for these products. The Firm has not experienced and does not anticipate, that all available lines of credit would be used at the same time. For credit card and home equity commitments (if certain conditions are met), the Firm can reduce or cancel theses lines of credit by providing the borrower notice or, in some cases, without notice as permitted by law.
(d) Receivables from customers primarily represent margin loans to retail brokerage customers, which are included in accrued interest and accounts receivable on the Consolidated Balance Sheets.
(e) Includes accrued interest and fees net of an allowance for the uncollectible portion of accrued interest and fee income.
(f) At December 31, 2013 and 2012, nonaccrual loans excluded: (1) mortgage loans insured by U.S. government agencies of USD 8.4 billion and USD 10.6 billion, respectively, that are 90 or more days past due: and (2) student loans insured by U.S. government agencies under the FFELP of USD 428 million and USD 525 million, respectively, that are 90 or more days past due. These amounts have been excluded from nonaccrual loans based upon the government guarantee. In addition, the Firm's policy is generally to exempt credit card loans from being placed on nonaccrual status as permitted by regulatory guidance.
(g) Excludes PCI loans. The Firm is recognizing interest income on each pool of PCI loans as they are all performing.
(h) Charge-offs and net charge-off rates for the year ended December 31, 2012, included incremental Chapter 7 loan net charge-offs of $91 million for senior lien home equity, $539 million for junior lien home equity, $47 million for prime mortgage, including option ARMs, $70 million for subprime mortgage and $53 million for auto loans. Net charge-off rates for the year ended December 31, 2012, excluding these incremental net charge-offs would have been 0.90%, 3.03%, 0.58%, 4.65% and 0.28% for the senior lien home equity, junior lien home equity, prime mortgage, including option ARMs, subprime mortgages and auto loans, respectively. See Consumer Credit Portfolio on pages 120–129 of this Annual Report for further details.
(i) Net charge-offs and net charge-off rates excluded $53 million of write-offs of prime mortgages in the PCI portfolio for the year ended December 31, 2013. See Consumer Credit Portfolio on pages 120–129 of this Annual Report for further details.
(j) Average consumer loans held-for-sale were $209 million and $433 million, respectively, for the years ended December 31, 2013 and 2012. These amounts were excluded when calculating net charge-off rates.

FIGURE 3.15 JPMorgan Chase's Consumer Credit Portfolio
Source: JP Morgan Chase 2013 Annual Report

Commonly reported risk items are loan-to-value (LTV) and FICO scores (see Chapter 2). With risky portfolios, such as the following Purchased Credit-Impaired (PCI) illustration, LTV numbers are particularly high.

December 31, (in millions, except ratios)	2013 Unpaid principal balance USD	Current estimated LTV ratio [a]	Net carrying value [c]	Ratio of net carrying value to current estimated collateral value [c]	2012 Unpaid principal balance USD	Current estimated LTV ratio [a]	Net carrying value [c]	Ratio of net carrying value to current estimated collateral value [c]
Home equity	$ 19,830	90% [b]	$ 17,169	78%	$ 22,343	111% [b]	$ 19,063	95%
Prime mortgage	11,876	83	10,312	72	13,884	104	11,745	88
Subprime mortgage	5,471	91	3,995	66	6,326	107	4,246	72
Option ARMs	19,223	82	17,421	74	22,591	101	18,972	85

(a) Represents the aggregate unpaid principal balance of loans divided by the estimated current property value. Current property values are estimated at least quarterly based on home valuation models that utilize nationally recognized home price index valuation estimates; such models incorporate actual data to the extent available and forecasted data where actual data is not available.

(b) Represents current estimated combined LTV for junior home equity liens, which considers all available lien positions, as well as unused lines, related to the property. All other products are presented without consideration of subordinate liens on the property.

(c) Net carrying value includes the effect of fair value adjustments that were applied to the consumer PCI portfolio at the date of acquisition and is also net of the allowance for loan losses at December 31, 2013 and 2012 of USD 1.8 billion and USD 1.9 billion for home equity, USD 1.7 billion and USD 1.9 billion for prime mortgage, USD 494 million and USD 1.5 billion for option ARMs, and USD 180 million and USD 380 million for subprime, respectively.

FIGURE 3.16 JPMorgan's Purchased Credit-Impaired Loans
Source: JP Morgan Chase 2013 Annual Report

3.7.3 Credit Losses

US banks publish allowances for credit losses, which is a convenient way of preparing shareholders for the possibility of credit losses. These are expected amounts, not yet confirmed.

If actual losses do not exceed these numbers, the bank is outperforming its originally reported expectations. This may result in an increase in the bank's stock price.

Year ended December 31, (in millions, except ratios)	2013 Consumer excluding credit card	2013 Credit Card	2013 Wholesale	2013 Total	2012 Consumer excluding credit card	2012 Credit Card	2012 Wholesale	2012 Total
Allowance for loan losses								
Beginning balance at January 1,	$ 12,292	$ 5,501	$ 4,143	$ 21,936	$ 16,294	$ 6,999	$ 4,316	$ 27,609
Gross charge-offs	2,754	4,472	241	7,467	4,805[d]	5,755	346	6,101
Gross recoveries	(847)	(593)	(225)	(1,665)	(508)	(811)	(524)	(1,843)
Net charge-offs/ (recoveries)	1,907	3,879	16	5,802	4297[d]	4,944	(178)	9,063
Write-offs of PCI loans[a]	53	-	-	53	-	-	-	-
Provision for loan losses	(1,872)	2,179	(119)	188	302	3,444	(359)	3,387
Other	(4)	(6)	5	(5)	(7)	2	8	3
Ending balance at December 31,	$ 8,456	$ 3,795	$ 4,013	$ 16,264	$ 12,292	$ 5,501	$ 4,143	$ 21,936
Impairment methodology								
Asset-specific[b])	$ 601	$ 971	$ 181	$ 1,753	$ 729	$ 1,681	$ 319	$ 2,729
Formula-based	3,697	2,824	3,832	10,353	5,852	3,820	3,824	13,496
PCI	4,158	-	-	4,158	5,711	-	-	5,711
Total allowance for loan losses	$ 8,456	$ 3,795	$ 4,013	$ 16,264	$ 12,292	$ 5,501	$ 4,143	$ 21,936
Allowance for lending-related commitments								
Beginning balance at January 1,	$ 7	$ -	$ 661	$ 668	$ 7	$ -	$ 666	$ 673
Provision for lending-related commitments	1	-	36	37	-	-	(2)	(2)
Other	-	-	-	-	-	-	(3)	(3)
Ending balance at December 31,	$ 8	$ -	$ 697	$ 705	$ 7	$ -	$ 661	$ 668
Impairment methodology								
Asset-specific	$ -	$ -	$ 60	$ 60	$ -	$ -	$ 97	$ 97
Formula-based	8	-	637	645	7	-	564	571
Total allowance for lending-related commitments	$ 8	$ -	$ 697	$ 705	$ 7	$ -	$ 661	$ 668
Total allowance for credit losses	$ 8,464	$ 3,795	$ 4,710	$ 16,969	$ 12,299	$ 5,501	$ 4,804	$ 22,604

FIGURE 3.17 JPMorgan Chase's Note on Credit Allowances
Source: JP Morgan Chase 2013 Annual Report

At the end of 2013, JP Morgan Chase made total allowances for consumer credit losses of around USD 12.3 billion (consumer, excluding credit card, of USD 8.5 billion and credit card of USD 3.8 billion) and for wholesale losses of USD 4.7 billion. In its 2007 Annual Report, the bank showed allowances for consumer credit losses of USD 6 billion and wholesale losses of USD 4 billion. Wholesale loss allowances are 20% higher, but the consumer credit number is over 105% higher in 2013, confirming that the 2008 financial crisis hit consumers—and consumer credit—disproportionately hard.

3.8 External Credit and Loan Review

The external review of a bank's credit processes, credit portfolio, and credit strategy is an integral part of the credit portfolio management process. While this external review is part of the supervisory review process, banks routinely rely on external reviewers and their analysis to help in assessing the quality of the bank's own internal credit processes. In fact, for many large banks with complex operations and sophisticated underwriting practices, the external loan review is a core tool in providing governance information about the credit process. The bank's management and board benefit from periodic and objective external loan reviews, which also help the leadership of the institution with regulatory compliance.

The results of the loan review are typically shared with senior management and with the board. Board level risk, audit, and credit committees are the typical consumers of external loan reviews.

3.8.1 Coverage of the Loan Review

While for smaller banks the loan review may contain all loans that have been underwritten, for larger banks the loan review may only focus on loans over a certain size, or a random sample of loans.

The loan reviewer analyzes the entire credit file, from the credit application, through the credit analysis, to the credit memorandum. In many cases, the loan review process is an extension of the regularly conducted internal audit of the bank's loan files. Both the loan reviewer and the internal auditors review the completeness of the loan files, looking to see that all relevant and required steps of the loan process have been completed and adequately documented. Documents that relate to the perfection of a bank's position with respect to collateral support typically receive intense scrutiny.

Having analyzed, reviewed, and scrutinized the individual loan files, the reviewers offer their professional opinion of the loan portfolio and individual loans. The reviewer may also offer suggestions to improve internal processes and practices. In some cases, the loan reviewer may suggest that certain loans should be rated differently, sold, or classified in a different manner.

3.8.2 Analyzing Risk-Rating Methodologies

Integral to the loan review is a review of the bank's loan rating methodologies. Here, the review focuses on the accuracy of individual risk ratings and on the effectiveness of the overall risk analysis system relative to the risk profile of the bank.

The chief problem arises when a bank's rating systems underestimate risk, because the ratings then convey inaccurate information and so impede credit portfolio management, as well as underestimating both the allowance of loan losses and regulatory capital requirements. It is particularly important to assess the nature and pattern of rating inaccuracies, especially when larger and riskier exposures are concerned.

For more quantitatively driven risk models, the model's performance under different situations should also be analyzed. These rating methodologies should be analyzed to ensure that they differentiate risk, are consistent in assigning risk grades, and remain consistent with lending standards and policies for handling all borrowers, including borrowers that do not pay as agreed. Furthermore, these quantitative models should also be designed to understand and replicate the assignment of grades using standardized information.

3.8.3 Stress Testing

Stress testing is an integral part of any bank's credit risk management procedures. It is a tool that is continuously evolving and regulators are increasingly relying on stress tests as an approach to quantify the risks of the bank, including those risks that may not be readily and easily seen unless credit conditions fundamentally change.

Through stress tests, a bank's management and regulators are able to quantify adverse and unexpected outcomes on the credit portfolio and capital levels. As stress tests focus on significant risk events, the outcome of a credit portfolio stress test often provides an estimate of additional capital requirements needed to sustain credit losses. Stress tests are hypothetical and contain a range of different "what-if" scenarios with different degrees of severity.

3.9 Summary

This chapter extended the credit risk assessment framework from the previous two chapters and considered how credit exposures are aggregated to compute portfolio risk measures. It also presented a detailed example of portfolio credit reporting from JPMorgan Chase.

Credit risk management

- Credit risk management seeks to ensure that banks operate safely, soundly, and prudently by creating strict standards for credit assessment and credit management.
- While initially credit risk management was an integral part of each bank's proprietary business model, in recent years the transparency of credit risk management has increased.
- The Basel Accords established international standards for credit risk capital requirements, and indirectly for credit risk management.
- Modern credit risk management relies on statistical and mathematical models.

Correlation in credit analysis

- It is easy to speak of correlation in credit events, but difficult to make use of it as a factor in credit analysis.
- Many banks use common risk factors to induce correlation among default events, such as regional unemployment affecting the PD of numerous retail borrowers simultaneously.
- Other banks use a copula technique to discern default correlations. This directly induces correlation but requires a very large number of parameters to represent pairwise correlations among obligors.
- In the copula model, many banks use constant correlations among obligors within each class and between classes.

Portfolio measures of credit risk

- The portfolio-credit-loss distribution is a negatively skewed distribution.
- Expected loss (EL) is a calculation of the expected losses on a credit portfolio level.
- Unexpected loss (UL) is the maximum loss expressed at a given level of statistical confidence.
- Credit value at risk (CVaR) is the difference between UL and EL.
- Where possible, it is desirable to know the influence of macroeconomic variables on the loss distribution.

- Aggregation methods include formulaic aggregations of simplified exposures, or complex simulations of joint default.

Managing the risk of the credit portfolio

- Banks are concerned with the amount of credit risk being taken, the return on capital for taking credit risk, alternative returns on capital, and concentration risk at the portfolio level.
- At the individual level, banks are concerned with their appetite, expertise, and resources to manage particular exposure types.
- Securitization is a way to bundle credit obligations and sell them, removing them from the balance sheet.
- Securitization can be a profit center in its own right. It also frees up both cash capital and risk capital for the bank to re-deploy.
- Credit derivatives such as credit default swaps can be used to remove some credit exposures from the bank's credit portfolio.
- Basic credit default swaps (CDSs) require a payment of a premium from the protection buyer in exchange for a make-whole payment on a reference debt instrument in the event of default. Therefore a bond plus a CDS is approximately a risk-free instrument, except for the credit quality of the CDS protection seller.

Credit portfolio management models

- Banks use various complex models to quantify their credit risk exposures.
- These models seek to quantify the likelihood and the potential value effect of a credit event, such as non-payment or bankruptcy (default risk), a downgrade in internal or external credit ratings (migration risk), a change in the price of credit without a change in the underlying credit rating (spread risk), or changes in the value of collateral and recoverability (recovery risk).
- These quantitative models can be distinguished according to whether they are transaction-driven or global, default or credit-value models, and how they consider macroeconomic effects and default-probability modeling.
- The results of these credit risk models can be used for loan pricing, risk-adjusted performance measurement, maximizing the risk and return trade-off of the portfolio, and establishing risk limits.

Problem asset management

- Banks often encounter credit losses, and they have developed skills to manage problem assets through workout teams and specialized asset management companies (bad banks).
- Workouts are complex processes with a range of different constituents, and banks must pay attention to the often-conflicting interests of these parties.

External credit and loan review

- The external credit and loan review is part of the governance process.
- By analyzing individual loans, loan portfolios, and underwriting criteria, the bank and its management can feel comfortable with how the credit risk—the chief risk of the bank—is being managed.

CHAPTER 4

The Regulatory View of Credit Risk

The final chapter of this book focuses on the regulatory view of credit risk as outlined by the Basel Accords. These Accords are international agreements between national banking supervisors representing large, developed countries; they provide wide-ranging recommendations on banking regulations. Their main focus is to link the risk of a bank's assets and operations to its capital levels, with bank capital levels increasing as the risk of the bank's overall operations increase. The Accords include Basel I, II, and III and they seek to ensure that banks have sufficient equity capital reserves available to cover risks. Section 4.7 outlines updated guidance on leveraged lending from US regulatory agencies: The Federal Reserve, Office of the Comptroller of the Currency (OCC), and the Federal Deposit Insurance Corporation (FDIC).

On completion of this chapter the reader will have an improved understanding of:

- Risk-based capital regulation focusing on establishing a direct relationship between a bank's risks and its equity and capital to ensure that banks operate safely, soundly, and prudently.
- The Basel Committee on Banking Supervision (BCBS), a committee of banking supervisory authorities which formulates supervisory standards and guidelines and recommends best practice in banking supervision.

The Basel Accords (I, II, and III) have evolved to serve as an international framework of banking supervisory rules that are broadly followed by regulators and supervisors across the world.

- The Basel Accords' two approaches for credit risk management: the Standardized Approach and the Internal Ratings Based (IRB) Approach.
- The requirements of the IRB Approach that a bank must include a number of considerations such as data accuracy, model calibration, and the impact of collateral in its IRB models.
- The Accords' specific rules pertaining to the supervision of securitization including a new framework under Basel III to address concerns that Basel II was overly reliant on external models and its risk weighting was poorly calibrated.
- Basel III's securitization framework, which is simpler, broadly consistent with the underlying framework for credit risk, and based on a hierarchy of three levels.
- US regulatory agencies'—the Federal Reserve, the Office of the Comptroller of the Currency and the Federal Deposit Insurance Corporation—guidance regarding leveraged credit products; banks and financial institutions operating under their jurisdiction must adhere to this guidance.

4.1. Linking Capital and Credit Risk

Risk-based capital regulation focuses on establishing a direct relationship between the bank's risks and the bank's equity and capital to ensure that banks operate safely, soundly, and prudently. The objective is to ensure the safety of the banking system by reducing the chance of bank failure. A bank that takes on more risk is believed to be at a greater risk of failing. Consequently, riskier banks should have more capital available to absorb potential losses. The deeper a bank's capital cushion to absorb losses, the less likely it becomes that the bank will default and imperil the funds of depositors and others.

The relationship between risk and capital in a risk-sensitive capital requirement framework, such as the Basel Accords, is determined by its two main components: the level of risk and the level of capital.

The various risks impacting a bank, such as credit, operational, market, liquidity, strategy, legal, business, etc., must be measured and quantified. To do so, numerous risk measurement and management systems have been developed and put in place. These systems calculate the risk exposure of the specific risks, and when necessary they convert the quantitative estimate of risk into a risk indicator, which can be an asset which is risk-weighted appropriately (credit risk) or the risk capital requirement for a specific risk (market risk and operational risk).

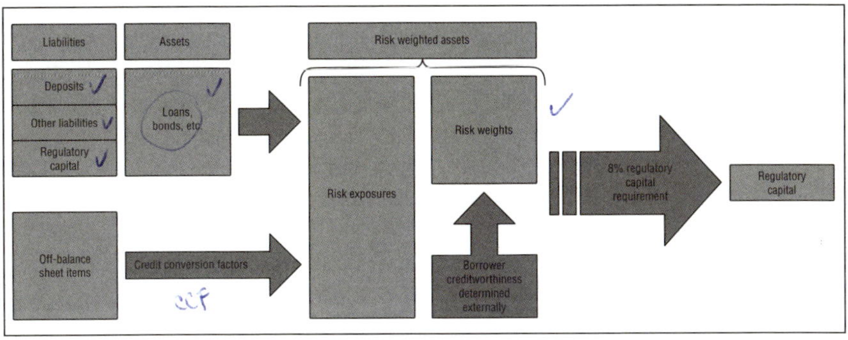

FIGURE 4.1 Linking Credit Risk with Capital Requirements

A bank should have sufficient levels of capital available to absorb these risks: sufficient from the perspective of regulators (regulatory capital) and for the economic consequences of these risks (economic capital).

4.1.1 Capital Levels Matter

At its core, a bank's capital is the owners' original capital contributions increased through subsequent capital contributions to the bank, either as newly raised capital or as earnings retained and added to the shareholders' original equity. Equity capital is expensive and sometimes difficult to raise, so it is often supplemented with other types of capital from secondary financing sources. These capital sources also include various types of debt, innovative instruments such as hybrid debt, and bank reserves such as disclosed or non-disclosed earnings.

For a small and even mid-size bank, where the board and management are large direct owners of the bank and are the primary source of capital, increased risk would directly translate to increased capital requirements. Alternatively, the increased risk would enhance the probability that the bank suffers from debilitating losses that imperil its long-term survivability. Thus, any bank that elects to pursue a riskier strategy by investing in riskier products would have to hold more equity against these increased risks. For a smaller bank, where the core source of capital is management and the board, this may not always be a feasible or practical solution, and thus such a bank is more likely to pursue strategic objectives and options that are limited by its access to equity. Here, capital regulation tends to work well.

4.2 The Evolution of the Basel Accords

Historically, banking regulation was national. Regulatory agencies developed rules and banking supervisory guidelines specific to each country's needs, and rules differed significantly between countries. Now, there is an international framework, coordinated by the Basel Committee on Banking Supervision (BCBS) and implemented by national regulators. As a forum of regulatory cooperation, the Basel Committee formulates broad banking supervisory standards, such as the Basel Accords, and develops guidelines for both banks and regulators.

In the mid-1980s, the Basel Committee recognized an overriding need to strengthen the international banking system's ability to withstand shocks. It introduced a system to help banks better assess their level of risk across all assets by establishing weightings based on the perceived relative credit risk associated with each asset. This more risk-sensitive balance sheet was weighted by risk factors that were broadly specific to credit instruments. The Basel Committee believed that this new framework, the Basel I Accord, would improve the safety and soundness of individual banks, and by extension, both national and international banking systems. By explicitly linking capital requirements to the asset risk of a bank, the new framework was believed to provide the right incentives to curb excessive risk taking. This Accord embraced the view, long advocated by policymakers, bankers, regulators, and academics alike, that as a bank takes on more risks, it should have more capital available to absorb possible losses.

4.2.1 The Basel I Accord

The Basel I Accord (Basel I) linked regulatory capital (RC) to risk-weighted assets (RWA). Regulatory Capital under the Accord consisted of Tier 1 and Tier 2 capital. Tier 1 capital is the key element of capital that supervisors place the most emphasis on and is the equity capital of the bank. Initially, only equity capital—paid in capital, retained earnings—and certain disclosed and after-tax reserves were included in these "core capital" calculations.

Starting in 1998, in a bid to reflect changes and innovation in the financial markets, the Basel Committee allowed the use of certain types of "innovative" capital as Tier 1 capital. Innovative Tier 1 capital consists of various financial instruments with both debt and equity features. In case a bank is liquidated, the innovative capital would be paid back after all the depositors and other creditors with higher repayment priority have been fully satisfied, but before shareholders are repaid. Due to the structural complexity of this source of capital, supervisors placed strict rules on the features of such market instruments and the extent to which they could be issued.

Tier 2 capital consists of certain undisclosed pre-tax reserves and subordinated debt. During liquidation, subordinated debt ranks in repayment below deposits and other credit, but above equity.

Under Basel I, the RWA was determined by the credit risk exposure of the bank; the method used to determine the size of the RWA was crude by contemporary standards. A simple set of different multipliers (known as risk weights) for government, bank, corporate, and personal debt was multiplied by an overall 8% target capital ratio; this was to be implemented by the end of 1992 in the member states.

These risk weights were based primarily on the nature of the borrower, e.g., corporate or OECD bank, and the type of instrument, e.g., a loan, guarantee, etc., or the asset class. The risk weights used were 0%, 10%, 20%, 50% and 100%. Figure 4.2 provides an abbreviated version.

0% Risk weight	20% Risk weight	50% Risk weight	100% Risk weight
Cash and cash equivalents Claims on central banks and central governments of OECD countries Government bonds issued by OECD countries (sovereign debt)	Claims on multilateral development banks (ADB) Claims on banks in OECD countries Claims on public entities in OECD countries	Loan secured by mortgages on residential property	Claims on the private sector Claims on central banks and central governments outside of OECD countries Other fixed assets of the bank

FIGURE 4.2 Selected Indicative Basel I Risk Weights
Source: International Convergence of Capital Measurement and Capital Standards, Annex 2, July 1988, BCBS

Subsequently, this common capital framework was introduced progressively in countries with active international banks, and in some countries these rules were applied uniformly across all banks, irrespective the geographical scope of their business activities.

EXAMPLE

The associated risk weight for a loan to a bank domiciled in an OECD country is 20%. For a USD 10 million loan, the risk-weighted assets are USD 2 million (= USD 10 million × 20%), and the regulatory capital requirement is USD 160,000 (= USD 2 million × 8%).

The associated risk weight for a loan to a bank not domiciled in an OECD country is 100%. For a USD 10 million loan, the risk-weighted assets are USD 10 million (USD 10 million × 100%), and the regulatory capital requirement is USD 800,000 (USD 10 million × 8%).

Linking risk with capital has become a well-established approach to quantify the relationship between the aggregate risk level of a bank and the capital supporting these risks levels.

4.2.2 Shortcomings of Basel I

Although hailed as a major step in international regulatory cooperation, Basel I had several severe shortcomings that limited its application and initially led to changes and extensions to the Accord, and eventually to the Basel II Accord (Basel II).

First, Basel I focused only on credit risk. Market, counterparty, currency, maturity mismatch, liquidity, and interest rate risks were ignored. To remedy some of these shortcomings, the Basel Committee in 1996 proposed the Market Risk Amendment that focused on the measurement of market risks and the capital to be held against market risks. Operational risks were not explicitly considered until Basel II, which also indirectly considered other hard-to-measure risks, such as liquidity risks and strategy risks.

Second, Basel I did not consider the connection between credit risk and maturity. Typically, short-term loans are believed to carry lower exposure levels than long-term loans due to the shorter time to payoff. Loans with longer maturity are riskier, because there is a greater window for these loans to default, for credit risk migration, or credit quality deterioration.

Third, Basel I did not appropriately differentiate across the various gradations of credit risk. The Accord gave the same RWA weighting of 100%, and thus imposed identical capital requirements, to all corporate loans irrespective of the credit rating of the borrower. This led to the unintended consequence that a bank investing in a AAA- or a BB-rated loan would be required to keep the same capital available, even though the probability of default—and the yield earned—is considerably higher for the BB-rated loan. Consequently, a bank had incentive to underwrite BB-rated loans, because it could charge higher interest rates, but only needed to reserve the same capital as it would against loans of much higher credit quality. Additionally, exposures to non-OECD countries were considered more risky than exposures to OECD countries.

EXAMPLE

A loan to an AAA-rated borrower, with a low risk of default, might carry an interest rate of 50 bp over comparable government bonds. A loan to a non-investment-grade borrower rated BB, with considerable risk of default, might carry an interest rate of 350 bp over comparable government bonds.

For a USD 10 million loan to an AAA-rated and a BB-rated borrower, the risk-weighted assets are the same at USD 10 million (= USD 10 million × 100%). Yet, the loan to the BB-rated borrower would earn a 300 bp margin over the loan to the AAA-rated borrower, or USD 300,000 more each year.

Fourth, Basel I failed to account for correlation, diversification, and risk reduction effects. The Accord demanded the same regulatory capital for a loan portfolio concentrated in one sector (such as an industrial sector or a geographical sector) as for a portfolio spread across different sectors. The risk reducing impact of a diversified credit portfolio with low correlation was not recognized by the Accord. This provided no specific incentive for banks to diversify their credit portfolios. As a result, banks did not need to proactively manage their credit risk exposures. By better recognizing risk mitigants and risk exposures, a bank can improve the management of the overall risk of its portfolios, as the cost of holding capital is reduced.

Finally, Basel I did not recognize the benefits that various risk reduction tools could offer. This is related to the lack of recognition of credit risk offsets. Initially, the benefits from the use of collateral, credit guarantees, and netting to reduce credit risk exposures were not part of the Accord, and explicit consideration for these tools only came as later extensions to the Accord.

4.2.3 The Development of Basel II

In 1999 the Basel Committee started working closely with the major banks of member countries to develop a new capital accord, Basel II. The general aim was to encompass all banking risk within a new comprehensive capital adequacy framework.

Work on developing Basel II coincided with moves in the European Union (EU) to harmonize its financial markets with the ultimate objective of creating an integrated trans-European financial market. Harmonization of banking and financial regulation across the EU was the first step. Given that a substantial number of the Basel Committee's members were also members of the EU, any changes to the existing risk-based regulatory framework would potentially impact the creation of an integrated financial market in the EU. Thus, Basel II could serve as basis for EU legislation on capital regulation of banks and financial services companies that were not internationally active. In fact, Basel II, with minor alterations, became the basis for a new EU directive on capital adequacy: the Capital Requirements Directive (CRD).

In 2004, after lengthy consultations, the new capital framework, Basel II, was published. It was first implemented in 2007. It consists of three pillars, as described below and in Figure 4.3.

Pillar 1

This sets minimum capital requirements, and is designed to improve upon the standardized rules in the 1988 Accord (Basel I). These minimum regulatory capital requirements reflect the three major types of risk that a bank faces: credit risk, market risk, and operational risk. The approach in Basel II cures some of the deficiencies in Basel I. Under Pillar 1, a bank can choose from different alternatives of varying complexity to calculate its minimum regulatory capital requirements. Basel II also represents the first attempt to assign a regulatory capital charge to the management of operational risk.

Pillar 2

This complements and strengthens Pillar 1 by establishing a prudential supervision process. It covers all the risks in Pillar 1 and adds some other considerations:

- The bank's calculation of the amount of economic capital, the amount of capital a bank will require to survive during times of distress, to cover Pillar 1 risks. Economic capital is discussed extensively in Chapter 3 of *Asset and Liability Risk Management*, one of the other books in the GARP Financial Risk and Regulation series.
- The creation of a governance structure within a bank to ensure internal supervision and oversight from the board of directors and senior management.
- The banking supervisor's evaluation of a bank's own risk-profile level and the processes the bank used to determine that level.

Pillar 3

This outlines the effective use of market discipline as a lever to strengthen disclosure and encourage sound banking practices. Market discipline is public disclosure of a bank's financial condition to depositors and other interested parties, allowing them to assess the condition of the bank. Disclosure is the degree to which a bank or any company reveals its assets, liabilities, and/or inner workings. Disclosure affords the market—other banks, depositors, and borrowers—a better picture of a bank's overall risk position and allows a bank's counterparties to price and trade appropriately.

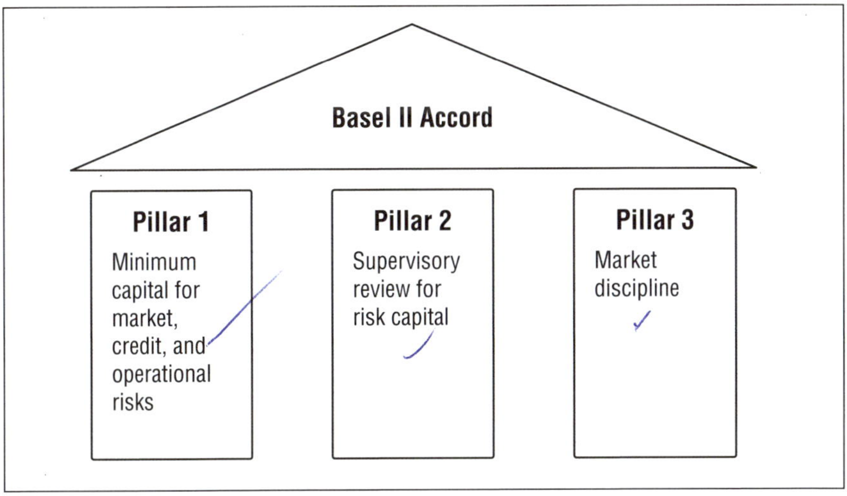

FIGURE 4.3 The Three Pillars of the Basel II Accord

The three pillars are intended to reinforce each other. The complex regulatory framework improves how regulatory capital requirements reflect underlying risks and addresses the effects of financial innovation.

During 2009, several changes to Basel II were published, in particular strengthening minimum capital requirements for certain securitization transactions and increasing risk weights for re-securitization exposures to better capture the inherent riskiness of these complex financial transactions. Due to the multi-layered complexity of these sophisticated credit products, a bank should conduct more rigorous credit analyses of externally rated securitization exposures.

4.2.4 The Basel III Framework

The global financial crisis of 2007-2009 highlighted the limitations of Basel II. Regulators, policy makers, and politicians took the opportunity to redesign, improve, and refine the architecture of the global financial system. The overriding objective of any newly proposed regulation was clear: it should reduce the likelihood that such a devastating crisis could recur in the future.

Following the global financial crisis, the Basel Committee for Banking Supervision (BCBS) was expanded to include all members of the G20. In addition, the Financial Stability Board (FSB) was set up in 2009 to monitor and make recommendations about the global financial system. The FSB consists of all G-20 major economies, the European Commission, BIS, World Bank, OECD, IMF, plus International standard-setting bodies (e.g., BCBS). It is hosted by the Bank for International Settlements.

In 2009 and 2010, the BCBS released a series of documents, amendments, and agreements to form "a comprehensive set of reform measures... to strengthen the regulation, supervision, and risk management of the banking sector." These documents amended and updated Basel II and altogether collectively formed Basel III. The framework was to be implemented incrementally and fully implemented by the end of 2018.

In the aftermath of the global financial crisis, risk management practices evolved and international regulation of financial institutions began to change as well. The significant stresses in the financial system helped identify weak points in the global financial system and its regulatory framework.

Basel III gives regulators the authority to monitor the health of individual banks and the interlinked network of international banks. In addition, it increases the capital requirements for individual banks, focusing on the ability to survive stress periods. It also includes new liquidity rules as well as introducing non-risk-based leverage limitations.

Whereas the two previous Basel Accords were micro-prudential, Basel III also includes macro-prudential provisions. Micro-prudential supervision focuses on the stability of the individual component parts of a financial system. Macro-prudential supervision focuses on the stability of a financial system as a whole.

Macro-prudential regulation recognizes that while individual banks may be working within the regulations, collectively their actions may result in the instability of a financial system. While maintaining the micro-prudential regulatory toolkit from Basel II that ensures the safe, sound, and prudent operations of banks, Basel III considers the effects of systemic risks that globally interconnected financial institutions propagate and seeks to address these risks.

Specifically with respect to credit risk management, Basel III seeks to protect the banking sector from periods of excess credit growth and reduces the risk that the supply of credit will be constrained during periods of financial stress.

4.2.5 Basel III Changes to Pillar I Risks

Basel III raises credit risk capital requirements in both the trading book and the banking book. With respect to re-securitization transactions, experience during the global financial crisis suggested that these sophisticated structures are particularly dependent on the availability of liquidity. For example, a typical re-securitization exposure is a CDO where the underlying asset pool consists of other CDOs, or a CDO^2 (pronounced "CDO squared"). Investors in the instrument receive the cash flow from other CDOs, thus the risk of the re-securitization exposure reflects the risk underlying each individual CDO and the risks of the assets included in the CDO.

To reflect these experiences, Basel III increases the capital requirements for banks active in this sector by:

- Adjusting the risk weight of re-securitization exposures in relation to the securitization exposures
- Harmonizing some credit conversion factors for specific liquidity facilities associated with securitization
- Demanding more rigorous credit analysis of externally rated securitization exposures
- Prohibiting the recognition of ratings that reflect guarantees or other support provided by banks

During the global financial crisis it became apparent that banks did not always understand the risks involved in a securitization, and that the quality and content of the underlying assets was not always clear. In addition there was an over reliance on credit rating agencies, so investors failed to perform their own due diligence or to ask questions about the riskiness of the securities they were purchasing.

To ensure banks carry out their own due diligence, they are required to do the following, on a continuous basis:

- Have a comprehensive understanding of the risk characteristics of their individual securitization exposures
- Be able to access performance information on the underlying pools in a timely manner
- Have a thorough understanding of all structural features of a securitization transaction that would materially impact the performance of the bank's exposures to the transaction

If the bank can show that it does these things, it may use the risk weights specified in the Basel II securitization framework.

To provide further stability to the financial system, Basel III enhances counterparty credit risk practices, including higher Pillar 1 capital requirements determined by stress tests. A bank must add a capital charge to cover the risk of mark-to-market losses on the expected counterparty risk to over-the-counter (OTC) derivatives. This is known as the credit value adjustments (CVA). These capital charges account for the effect of deteriorating credit quality on transactions with counterparties.

Some derivatives are traded on futures exchanges and others are traded on the OTC market. The OTC market is where banks trade directly with each other rather than through an exchange. By adding CVAs to OTC transactions, the regulations provide incentives for banks to execute derivative transactions through centralized exchanges and clearinghouses.

When trading derivatives through an exchange, the transaction is with a central counterparty (CCP). Under Basel III, exposures to qualifying CCPs are subject to very low capital charges, as they benefit from the multilateral netting and loss-mutualization mechanism provided by the CCP:

- Banks will qualify for a 0% to 2% risk weight for central counterparty risk exposure
- Transactions with a central counterparty are excluded from the CVA capital charge

4.3 Credit Risk: Standardized Approach

The Standardized Approach in Basel II has not been impacted by Basel III. It uses different risk weights for corporate, sovereign, and bank exposures depending on their external credit assessment. If a credit is not externally rated, Basel II mandates a 100% risk weighting, however this assumes that the national supervisor is confident that the 100% risk weighting adequately reflects the historical default experience of that specific type of exposure. In case of past due, non-accruing, and otherwise substandard loans, supervisors may demand risk weighting of up to 150%.

Basel I did not specifically differentiate retail exposures by providing risk weights other than 100%. Basel II introduces a specific risk weight for retail exposures, reducing the supervisory risk weight for retail credits to 75% and for residential real estate loans to 35%. Additionally, loans to Small and Medium-Sized Enterprises (SMEs) can be treated as retail loans under Basel II, as long as certain requirements are met. A summary of the weights is given in Figure 4.3.

	Credit Assessment						
Counterparty	**AAA to AA**	**A**	**BBB**	**B**	**Below B**	**Unrated**	**Past Due**
	%	%	%	%	%	%	%
Corporate	20	50	100	150	150	100	150
Sovereign Entity	0	20	50	100	150	100	
Banks (OECD)	20	50		100	150	50	
Banks (Non-OECD)	20	50	100		150	100	
Retail	75						
Residential Real Estate	35						100
Non-residential Real Estate	Between 50-150%, reflecting national discretion						150

FIGURE 4.4 Basel II Accord Risk Weights
Source: International Convergence of Capital Measurement and Capital Standards. A Revised Framework ("Basel II"), June 2006.

EXAMPLE

Bank E lends USD 3 million to a corporate customer. This corporate customer is graded A+ to A–. Under the Standardized Approach this loan is converted to a risk-weighted asset as follows:

Risk-weighted asset = USD 3 million × 50% = USD 1.5 million
Minimum capital required = Risk Capital (RC) = USD 1.5 million × 8% = USD 120,000.

One of the shortcomings of Basel I was the limited consideration given to credit risk mitigants, such as collateral, credit guarantees, and credit derivatives that can reduce potential exposure on individual credits in case of default. Basel II includes most types of financial instruments as eligible collateral. Different instruments provide different levels of credit support, and these are determined based on either a supervisory standard, i.e., haircuts, or the market risk of the instrument used as collateral.

The Standardized Approach to credit risk in Basel II is an improvement on Basel I, but lacks the sophistication of the more quantitative approaches that use banks' internal data. These more quantitative approaches are incorporated in the Internal Rating-Based Approaches described in Section 4.4.

In December 2014, the Basel Committee published a consultative document outlining its key considerations for changes to the Standardized Approach under Basel III.[7] Its main considerations were reducing the reliance on external ratings, increasing risk sensitivities, reducing national discretions, strengthening the link between the Standardized Approach and the IRB Approach, and enhancing the comparability of capital requirements among banks.

However, the consultation paper noted that sovereigns, central banks, and public sector entities were not considered within its scope. The Basel Committee said that it intended to review these as part of a broader review of sovereign-related risks.

4.3.1 Incorporating Public Debt Grades

Although three major credit ratings agencies dominate the market (Moody's Investors Service, Standard & Poor's, and Fitch Ratings), Basel II allows the use of credit ratings by any external rating agency as long as the ratings and the agency meet the following criteria.

- Objectivity: analytical techniques must be rigorous
- Independence: the institution must be free from political and economic pressure
- Transparency: rating methodologies must be publicly available and assessments be broadly available
- Disclosure: technical model factors such as the definition of default and the time horizon of assessments must be publicly disclosed
- Resources: the institution must ensure it has the expertise and information required

7 Basel Committee on Banking Supervision, Consultative Document, Standards, Revisions to the Standardized Approach for credit risk, December 22, 2014. Issued for comment on March 27, 2015.

- Credibility: from an internal perspective that the agency has defined criteria for assessing credit grades, and from an external perspective that there is widespread acceptance and use of the agency's grades.

In practice, rating agencies need to demonstrate to national supervisors that they fulfill these criteria in order for their ratings to be used by banks to calculate risk weightings on their exposures for regulatory purposes.

Basel II makes a specific allowance for Export Credit Agencies (ECAs) to grade claims on sovereign entities. The risk-scoring methodologies used must be the same as the criteria set out by the OECD. A bank can either use the assessment grades of individual ECAs or "consensus" grades published by ECAs that participate in the "Arrangement of Officially Supported Export Credits."

Basel II sets high standards for the inclusion of external ratings to determine capital requirements. Consequently, only a few developed countries may have sufficient rating information available to make this aspect of the Standardized Approach widely applicable to rate corporate debt. Furthermore, the public ratings that are available are largely limited to large corporate credits with publicly issued debt. This may account for the Internal Ratings Based (IRB) Foundation Approach proving popular as an alternative with many banks that wish to move towards a more risk-sensitive approach to lending.

4.3.2 Specific Risk-Weight Classification

In order to create a greater sensitivity to risk, the Standardized Approach under Basel II creates a grid based primarily on the credit standing of the borrower. It produces a series of risk weights mainly related to the public credit grade of the borrower, although there is still a reference back to the asset classes. This can be seen from the way the credit grades for different asset classes result in different risk weights.

Risk Weight of a Sovereign Lender or Central Bank

At the discretion of the national supervisor, this can be set as low as 0% as long as the exposure is a sovereign credit or a central bank exposure and is denominated in the domestic currency. This 0% risk weight can be applied irrespective of the sovereign's public grade.

Risk Weight of Bank Exposures

Two alternatives can be used to determine the risk weighting on exposures banks have to other banks.

- Option 1 requires that a claim on a bank should be rated one category below that of the sovereign where the bank is domiciled.
- Option 2 mirrors the approach for corporate loan exposures: the risk weight reflects the external rating of the bank. In the case of unrated banks, a 100% risk weighting applies. (This could be a serious problem for banks with exposures to small unrated banks.)

Securities firms can be treated as either bank or corporate exposures. If the securities firm is subject to a regulatory regime comparable to Basel II (including risk-based capital requirements) such claims are treated as claims on banks. If not, they are treated as claims on corporate borrowers.

Risk Weight on Retail and Small Business Exposures

Retail and small business exposures are weighted at 75% as long as they are included in a regulatory retail portfolio that includes certain types of exposure, such as revolving credits, credit cards, and credit lines, and personal term loans. This excludes a number of loan types that may be used by sole traders and small businesses.

The 75% risk weight for the regulatory retail portfolio does recognize that these exposures are typically the result of a very large number of well-diversified small exposures. Thus the likelihood of a significant number of these exposures proving problematic at the same time is reasonably low, and will primarily be dependent on macroeconomic conditions, such as interest rates and unemployment levels.

Risk Weight on Mortgage Exposures

Lending against residential property carries a risk weighting of 35%, as long as the loan is secured on property owned and occupied or rented out to others by the borrower. The risk-weighting reduction recognizes the high quality of mortgage-type lending and the quality of residential property as security for the loan.

Risk Weight of Bad Debts

The Basel II Standardized Approach in Figure 4.4 grid shows that counterparties rated below B are risk weighted at 150%. Typically, such loans may be close to default, which raises the issue of whether or not the bank has allocated an amount of its capital to recognize that the obligation, and/or interest due on it, will not be paid in full.

Under Basel II a 150% risk weighting must be applied to the obligation if:

- No specific provision has been allocated to the loan, and
- Either payment of principal or interest is more than 90 days overdue.

This may be reduced by the allocation of a specific provision to the obligation. The risk weight may be reduced to 100% if each specific provision is greater than 20% of the obligation's outstanding amount. The risk weight may be reduced to 50% if the specific provision allocated is over 50% of the outstanding amount.

The possibility of reducing the risk weightings allowed under Basel II incorporates the principle that a bank often expects some recovery of defaulted loans. The percentage of a loan obligation that a bank fails to recover in such circumstances is known as the LGD.

Risk Weighting of Off-Balance-Sheet Items

These are converted into credit exposure equivalents (loan equivalents) through the use of a credit conversion factor (CCF), where the conversion factor reflects the type of exposure and its maturity.

EXAMPLE

Of a USD 100,000 loan commitment, USD 40,000 is used and USD 60,000 remains unused. If this is a loan commitment with a maturity of one year, the CCF under the Accord is 20%. The loan equivalent amount of this item is then USD 12,000 (= USD 60,000 × 20%). The loan equivalent amount is multiplied by the supervisory risk weight to yield the RWA and the Required Capital (RC) associated with the commitment. If the supervisory risk-weight is 100%, then the RWA is USD 12,000 and the RC is 8% of the RWA, USD 960.

4.3.3 Collateral and Credit Mitigants

Basel II recognizes the risk mitigating impact of collateral used as a secondary source of repayment, and offers three approaches to reducing credit risk capital requirements due to the presence of collateral:

- The Simple Approach
- The Comprehensive Approach
- The Advanced Comprehensive Approach

Banks using the Standardized Approach to calculate their capital requirements for credit risk may use either the Simple or the Comprehensive Approach. The Advanced Comprehensive Approach can only be used by those banks that are allowed to use an IRB Approach. The specific rules for the Advanced Comprehensive Approach are described in Section 4.5.5.

The Simple Approach allows the bank to reduce the risk weight of the exposure backed by collateral by substituting the collateral's risk weight. To be able to do so, the collateral must be marked-to-market and revalued at least every six months, and typically includes publicly traded investment-grade bonds, equity traded on major exchanges, and government debt. For cash, certain government securities, or certain repo instruments, there is no risk-weight floor, but for others the floor or minimum value is 20%.

The Comprehensive Approach allows the bank to reduce the value of the exposure by a discounted value of the collateral, where this haircut reflects the credit rating of the collateral, the issuer, and the maturity.

EXAMPLE

Collateral consisting of AA-rated government debt, with a remaining maturity of five years or less, would be discounted by 4%. If a corporate bond were used as a collateral, the haircut would be 8%. Alternatively, regulatory agencies may permit a bank to calculate its own discounts based on internal models that take into account market volatility, historical performance, and foreign exchange rate movement.

Where a bank has legally enforceable netting arrangements, it may calculate capital on the basis of the net credit exposure. In addition, both guarantees and credit protection derivative contracts are recognized as long as certain requirements are met.

4.4 Credit Risk: Internal Ratings-based Approaches

Supplementing the Standardized Approach to calculate credit risk capital, Basel II allows two computationally more complex approaches that rely on the bank's own internal quantitative assessments of credit risk. These risk assessment calculations are based on advances in quantitative credit risk management methodologies that rely heavily on large-scale statistical analysis of risk.

The Internal Ratings-based (IRB) Approaches include a simpler, Foundation IRB, and a more sophisticated, Advanced IRB, Approach. The difference between these two approaches reflects what information is supplied by the supervisors and what information is estimated by the bank's internal risk models. Both the Foundation and the Advanced IRB Approaches focus on the correct assessment of four inputs in the credit risk models, which are:

- Probability of default (PD): measures the likelihood that the borrower will default over a given time horizon
- Loss given default (LGD): measures the proportion of the exposure that will be lost in the event of a default occurring
- Exposure at default (EAD): measures, for loan commitments, the amount of the facility that is likely to be drawn down in case of a default occurring
- Effective Maturity (M): measures the remaining economic maturity of the exposure

Based on this information, a bank using an IRB Approach would calculate the Expected Loss (EL) and Unexpected Loss (UL) on each credit exposure using PD, LGD and EAD. The formula to calculate EL can be written either as EL = PD * LGD * EAD or more simply as EL = PD * LGD. The former expresses EL as a loss specified in monetary terms (useful for a bank which has specific EAD information on its borrowers when estimating the value of its EL) whereas the latter expresses the loss simply as a percentage (used where EAD is not known or by users such as Credit Rating Agencies when they make comparative judgments on the creditworthiness of borrowers).

EL is the loss expected under normal business circumstances and is typically priced in the loan as a spread over a benchmark rate. But from a risk management and regulatory perspective, UL is more relevant; its estimation is discussed in Section 4.4.2.

The differences in the Foundation and Advanced IRB Approaches are shown in Figure 4.5.

Data input	Foundation IRB	Advanced IRB
PD	Provided and computed by the bank	Provided and computed by the bank
LGD	Supervisory values set either by the Basel Committee or banking supervisors if permitted by rules of national discretion	
EAD		
M		

FIGURE 4.5 Differences between IRB Approaches

4.4.1 Comparing the Various Methodologies

Basel II requires that regulatory capital be more sensitive to risk. The following graph exemplifies how the various methods of calculating capital are impacted as a result of Basel II. The two approaches under the Basel II Accord provide risk assessments with differing sensitivities. The capital requirements increase with a decrease in ratings grades in the Standardized Approach, but using the IRB Approaches, the capital requirements increase at a different rate.

The differences in risk sensitivities across these three approaches are perhaps the clearest on the two extreme ends of the risk spectrum. Highly rated loans with low expected-default rates demand relatively low capital requirements following Basel II rules. Low-rated loans with high expected-default rates demand substantially higher limited capital requirements.

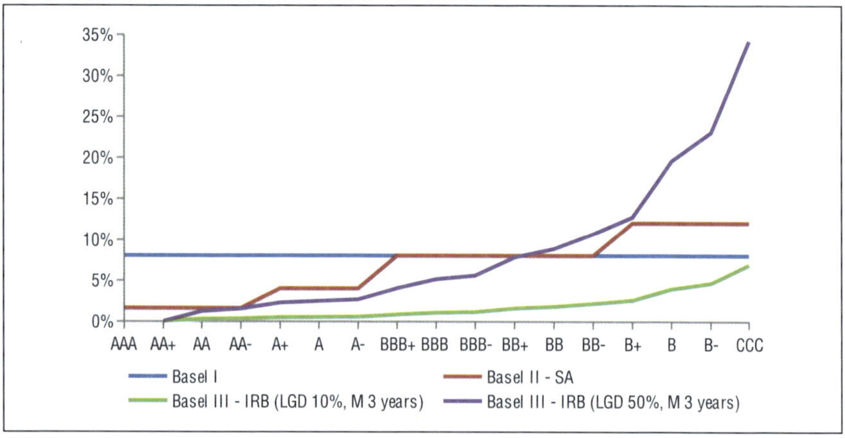

FIGURE 4.6 Capital Requirement for a Corporate Loan under the Basel Accords

The three approaches to calculate credit capital requirements differ in complexity and granularity. To compare the effects of these approaches, first the grading models and risk weight functions for various exposures are outlined. Figure 4.6 compares the risk weights from Basel I with the right weights in the Standardized Approach in Basel II and the IRB Approach under Basel III to analyze the differential impacts.

A bank that can, through its credit risk grading model, estimate a probability of default on the horizontal axis can then "read off" the appropriate risk weight on the vertical axis. This risk weight is then multiplied by the individual capital ratio (ICR) to give the regulatory capital requirement. Basel II in Annex 5 computes the various risk weights for some standardized exposures. The ensuing graphs illustrate the information provided in that Annex.

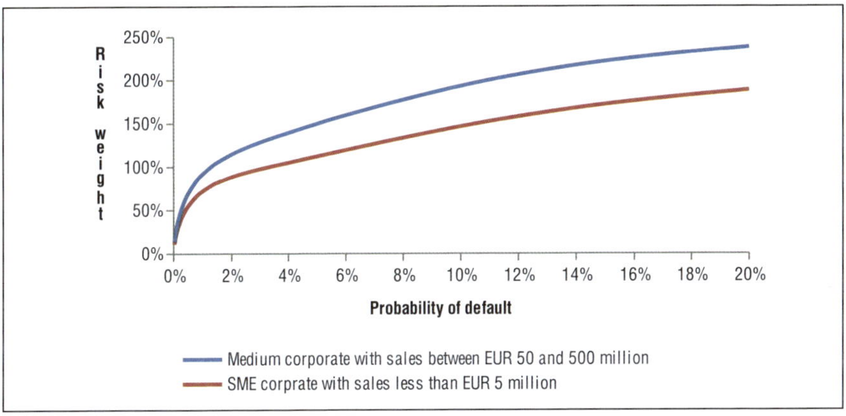

FIGURE 4.7 Risk Weights for Corporate Exposures LGD = 45%

Figure 4.7 depicts the risk curve for medium-sized enterprises with reported sales between EUR 50 million and EUR 500 million, and SMEs with reported sales of between EUR 5 million and EUR 50 million, and with exposure below EUR 1 million. It should be noted that large corporate entities with reported sales over EUR 500 million need to be calibrated on an individual basis.

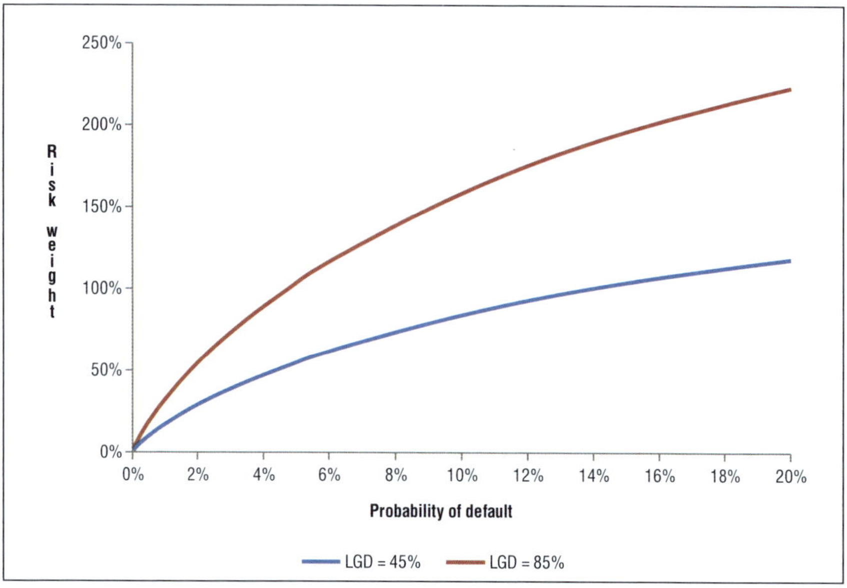

FIGURE 4.8 Risk Weights for Qualifying Revolving Retail Exposures

Figure 4.8 shows a risk curve for all revolving unsecured exposures to individuals that are uncommitted and unconditionally cancelable, involving a loss of under EUR 100,000 (LGD = 85% and LGD = 45%).

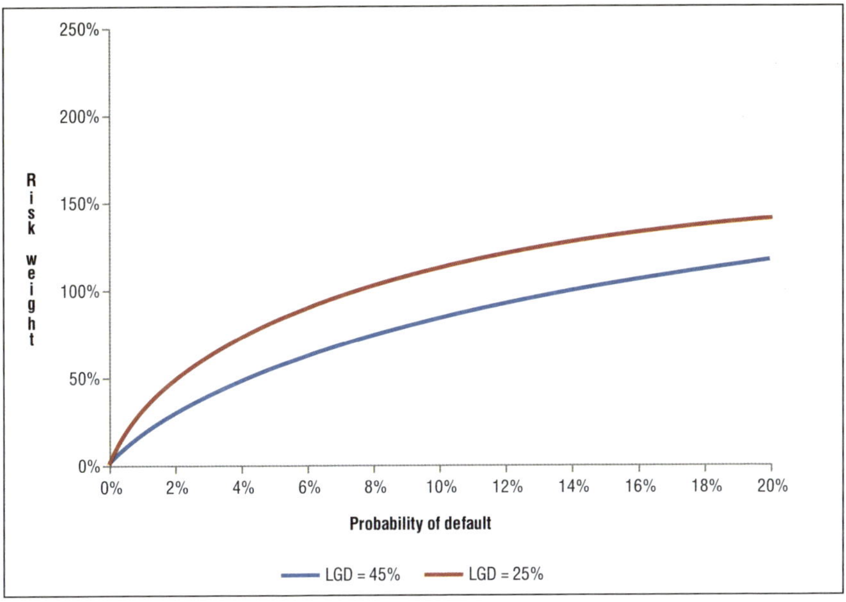

FIGURE 4.9 Risk Weights for Residential Mortgages

Figure 4.9 shows the risk curve for residential mortgages (LGD = 45% and LGD = 25%). Residential mortgages comprise all exposures secured on property by means of a mortgage or land charge on residential real estate.

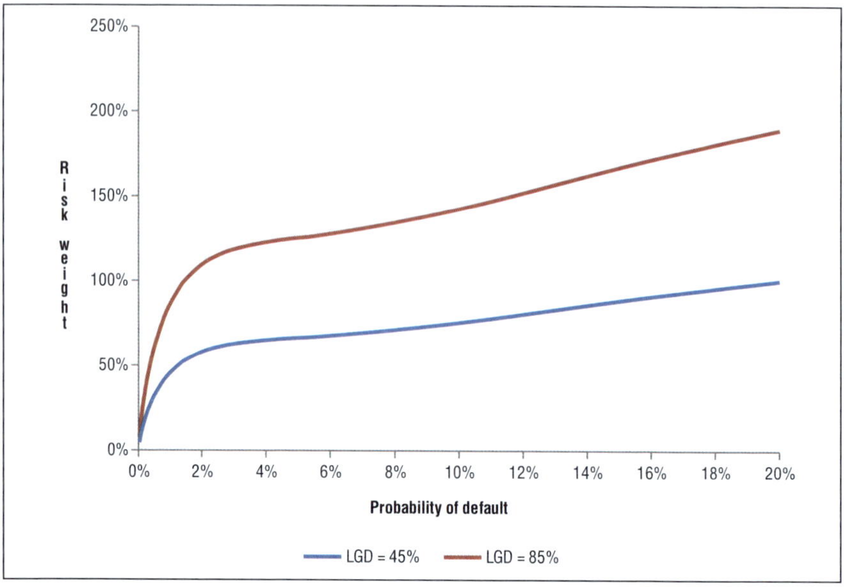

FIGURE 4.10 Risk Weights for Other Retail Exposures, (excluding Mortgages, etc.)

Finally, Figure 4.10 shows the risk curve for other retail exposures (LGD = 45% and LGD = 85%). Other retail exposures include all other loans to individuals and SMEs (below the corporate exposure qualifying criteria) not secured by mortgages on residential property.

4.4.2 The Idea behind the IRB Approaches

Although both the IRB and the Standardized Approaches link the credit risk of a bank's assets to the capital levels it should hold against these risks, the difference is that in the Standardized Approach the risk-weighted assets are calculated by fixed risk weights and the recorded value of the exposure.

The IRB Approaches are based on the concept of provisioning capital against UL, and assume that, given the risk level of the borrowers, the state of the economy, economic cycles, and various credit risk mitigants, average credit losses (i.e., EL) are reasonably easy to predict. Therefore EL can be considered a cost of a banking business; it should already be priced in and adequate provisions made in a bank's financial statements, either through provisions or reserves.

However, at times actual losses exceed EL, and then these losses become infrequent, but sizeable UL, as the graph shown in Figure 4.11 demonstrates.[8] If UL is unexpectedly large, then theoretically a bank's capital can be extinguished due to these losses, which from a regulatory safety and soundness perspective would require a bank to fully provision adequate capital against all its credit exposures. While possible, this would be an inefficient use of capital, but it would eliminate the concern of bank insolvency. Consequently, both banks and regulators face a trade-off: determining how much capital banks should have available given the possibility that loan losses could exceed expected loan loss levels, potentially eroding capital and leading to insolvency.

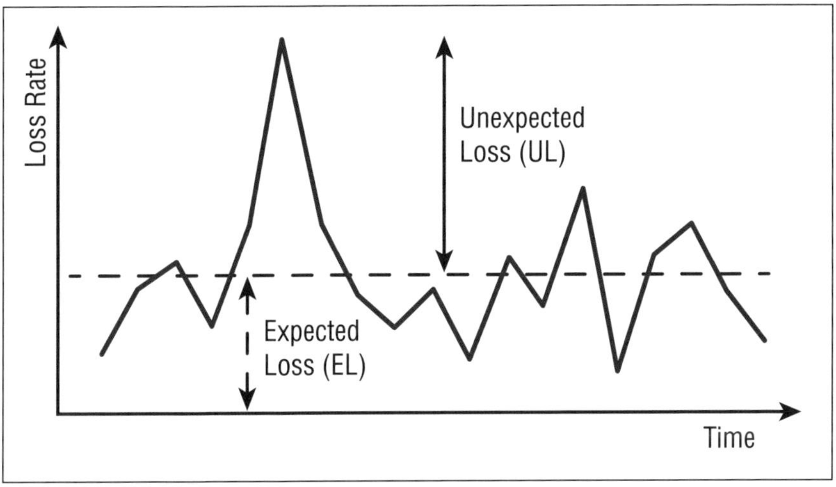

FIGURE 4.11 Loss Rate, Expected and Unexpected Losses

The IRB Approach sets UL as the capital requirement for a bank. As noted above, EL is covered through loan loss provisions as they are considered "normal."

To estimate UL, the IRB Approaches build on the assumption that the value of the borrower's assets depends on two factors, the systematic risk factor and the idiosyncratic risk factor. By extension, both the value of the loan on the balance sheet and the risk of the loan that a bank assumes depend on these two factors in terms of their direction, magnitude, and relationship or correlation. Chapter 3 offers a more detailed discussion of

8 Basel Committee on Banking Supervision: An Explanatory Note on the Basel II IRB Risk Weight Functions, July 2005, p 2.

correlation in credit risk measurement. The systematic risk factor impacts all exposures on a bank's books and could reflect economic performance, credit cycle, or other factors that would impact all exposures similarly. The idiosyncratic factor impacts are credit-or facility-specific, i.e., they solely impact that specific credit, exposure, or facility.

Although these two risk factors are not related to each other, their weights are linked. If the value of an asset falls under a certain threshold, caused by the movement of either systematic or idiosyncratic risk factors, or both, then there is a default. Based on the normal distribution the probability of when a default would occur can be easily modeled and computed. This metric would be the PD, one of the inputs in the IRB risk models. The other two core inputs are EAD, which gives an estimate of the amount outstanding, and LGD, which gives the percentage of exposure the bank might lose in case the borrower defaults. Based on the PD and the value of the asset adjusted for the loss in case of default, LGD, we can simply calculate EL. In other words, EL = PD × EAD × LGD.

Therefore in order to calculate UL, EL must be deducted from the overall loss, which is what the IRB risk-weight functions determine based on the PD, LGD, EAD, and M, adjusted for EL. The IRB capital requirement then needs to be adjusted for correlation and maturity. These adjustments are specific to various types of assets.

Capital requirements under IRB are set at very high levels of confidence, which means that these reflect highly unlikely events or have a very low PD. Often these highly unlikely events are considered stress events. In the IRB framework, the level of confidence is set at 0.1%, meaning that there is a one-in-a-thousand (0.1%) chance that there is a default, or a 99.9% chance that there is no default.[9] Based on the two-factor relationship that determines the value of the asset and the probability that an unlikely event would occur, we arrive at the relationship that quantifies the loss for one asset and thereby determines the UL: the capital requirement under the IRB Approaches.

4.4.3 The Foundation IRB Approach

In the Foundation IRB Approach it is only the PD of a borrower that is estimated by a bank's credit model. In addition, the PD must be set based on a minimum requirement of five years' relevant data. The LGD and the EAD are set by the national supervisors and will depend on the asset classes

9 By implication, a loan portfolio with 1,000 identical loans would suffer one loss over the time horizon, which is typically set at one year.

and collateral held by the bank. Effective maturity (M) is set at 2½ years (30 months), although M may also be set at the discretion of the national supervisor. Adjustments for collateral can be made.

For retail exposures, banks must provide their own estimate of PD, LGD, and EAD based on homogenous retail portfolio risk measures, and there is no distinction between the Foundation and the Advanced IRB Approaches for this asset class.

4.4.4 The Advanced IRB Approach

In the Advanced IRB Approach a bank must estimate all the relevant risk components, i.e., the PD, LGD, and EAD for all asset classes. Maturity and size factors do not require estimation as they can be computed from specific loan and exposure level data. The estimates used for these models must be based on a minimum requirement of seven years' data. National supervisors may allow a uniform 2½ year (30 months) assumption for effective maturity (M) for corporate exposure other than to large corporate loans, where M must be specific to the loan.

While there may appear to be a relatively minor difference between the Foundation and Advanced IRB Approaches, in practice the models that are needed to predict LGD and EAD (in addition to PD) are far more complex. Furthermore, the data requirements, calibration problems, and backtesting of an individual bank's model will be far more challenging under the Advanced IRB Approach than under the Foundation IRB Approach.

In addition, under the Advanced IRB Approach a bank may use a wide range of collateral to mitigate credit risk, including real estate, and may establish its own estimates of LGD based on the quality of its debt recovery processes.

4.4.5 Asset Class-Specific Requirements under IRB

Basel II explicitly considers the impact that credit risk mitigants may have on a bank's exposures and provides two alternative approaches to assess their effect. One of the approaches is similar to the building block approach in the Standardized Approach, where different types of assets have collateral weights determined by a supervisory formula. The second alternative considers a bank's own estimate of the risk of collateral based on VaR-like estimates.

EXAMPLE

Bank F extends a USD 10 million loan to an unrated corporate customer, who in return offers a high-quality financial asset with a value of USD 8 million as collateral. As the loan is unrated, the risk weight is 100%. RWA = USD 10 million and RC = USD 0.8 million (= RWA × 8%).

The collateral support of USD 8 million reduces the RWA to USD 2 million, and the RC falls to USD 0.16 million (= USD 2 million × 8%).

The degree of risk reduction associated with any risk mitigant depends directly on which IRB Approach the bank follows. Since the Advanced IRB Approach requires the estimate of the LGD parameter, it provides greater flexibility in comprehensively quantifying the effect of various credit risk mitigants on reducing credit risk. If the Foundation IRB Approach is used, supervisory estimates and assessments guide the effect the risk mitigant has on the LGD estimates of a specific exposure.

Basel II provides only an Advanced IRB Approach for calculating the credit risk exposure for retail credits. Unlike the approach followed for corporate, bank, and sovereign exposures, where the risk of each individual exposure is quantified separately, retail credit estimates are not based on individual exposures, but rather on pools of similar exposures. The Accord provides detailed specifications on the creation of these pools and how the particular requirements for the three main types of retail exposures—residential mortgages, qualifying revolving retail (credit cards), and other retail—need to meet.

Basel II also identifies five forms of more specialized forms of corporate lending. These are project finance, object finance, commodities finance, income-producing real estate, and high-volatility commercial real estate (HVCRE), where the risk weights can either reflect standard corporate lending credit ratings or certain supervisory quality grades. In case of HVCRE, a separate, more conservative risk-weight formula can be used.

Finally, the Accord requires banks with equity credit exposure using either of the two IRB Approaches to treat their equity exposures separately. Two alternatives are offered: one requires banks to estimate the PD of the equity exposure, and the other requires banks to estimate the potential decrease in market value.

4.5 Other Considerations

Before a bank can use either IRB Approach it must obtain supervisory approval through an on-site audit to establish compliance with and adherence to minimal qualitative and quantitative requirements set by the supervisor.

The minimum qualitative requirements ensure that a bank's IRB models are actually used to make credit risk management decisions. This is known as the usage test. A bank must not use its internal models simply to calculate credit risk for capital adequacy purposes. They must actually be used in the overall pricing and management of credit risk.

The quantitative minimum requirements are designed to ensure that a bank's estimates of PD, LGD, and EAD are reliable and accurate. This is done by validating the estimates of the bank's IRB risk components against actual defaults and losses.

For both approaches, the core requirement is that a bank's complex credit risk measurement, management, and monitoring system should be a ratings-based system that accurately captures the inherent riskiness of each loan in the bank's loan portfolio. Moreover, the system should be able to differentiate between individual loan exposures by correctly assessing the inherent riskiness of each loan relative to all the other loans. A model should have at least eight PD rating grades. Since the IRB Approaches both use complex statistical models, regulators should be able to validate a model by replicating the model's results. This should ensure that the models are reasonably accurate and consistent estimates of risk, and support lending decisions. The system should also dynamically provide information that allows for continuous reassessment and performance evaluation.

4.5.1 Grading and Accuracy

The ability of a grading model to accurately predict the PD of a counterparty can only be judged by looking at past data to assess how accurate model predictions have been. A model that has several grades will result in each grade covering a narrower range of PD estimates. While a grading model with a number of grades will purport to be more accurate than one with fewer grades, the assumed accuracy may prove to be illusory when tested against past data.

EXAMPLE

The table in Figure 4.12 lists both credit grades and associated PDs. The credit rating model has four grades covering AAA to AA and will need to discriminate between a PD of 0.01%, 0.02%, 0.03%, and 0.04%. However, if it had only one grade covering AAA to AA it would only need to discriminate between a PD above and below 0.04% to allocate a counterparty to the top grade.

As can be seen from Figure 4.12 PDs rise geometrically as credit grades fall. A bank therefore needs to monitor the migration of a counterparty should it move across credit grades over time. It is essential that the credit grades are reviewed at least annually.

Credit grade	PD
i_AAA	0.010%
i_AA+	0.020%
i_AA	0.030%
i_AA-	0.040%
i_A+	0.050%
i_A	0.070%
i_A-	0.090%
i_BBB+	0.140%
i_BBB	0.230%
i_BBB-	0.390%
i_BB+	0.640%
i_BB	1.070%
i_BB-	1.760%
i_B+	2.920%
i_B	4.820%
i_B-	7.950%
i_CCC+	13.000%

FIGURE 4.12 Sample Internal Credit Grades and Associated PDs

A number of approaches can be used to develop a grading model. A detailed description of the development of specific grading models is beyond the scope of this book, but typically relies on Credit VaR models as discussed in Chapter 3.

4.5.2 Backtesting of Model Results for Credit Grades

Backtesting the prediction capabilities of credit grading models is not a simple task even for Foundation IRB models. Credit losses are not uniform across time, rather, they are subject to the effects of business cycles. This means that companies and individuals will have far more problems paying interest and repaying the principal on their loans when the overall economy enters a cyclical downturn.

Economic downturns can have a strong adverse effect on both a borrower's ability to pay interest and principal as well as on the value of loan collateral. For example, if one housing loan defaults, the security (i.e., the house) is unlikely to change in value as a result of the default. If many similar loans default then many houses will be on the market and their value is likely to fall, adversely affecting the scale of loan losses. The cyclicality of credit and its impact has ramifications for the structure of all IRB models. There are two types of credit grading models. Through-The-Cycle (TTC) credit grading models attempt to estimate PD taking normal credit cycles into account. The alternative is the Point-In-Time (PIT) credit grading model that attempts to grade credits given the current state of the economy. Both models, depicted in Figure 4.13 have advantages and shortcomings.

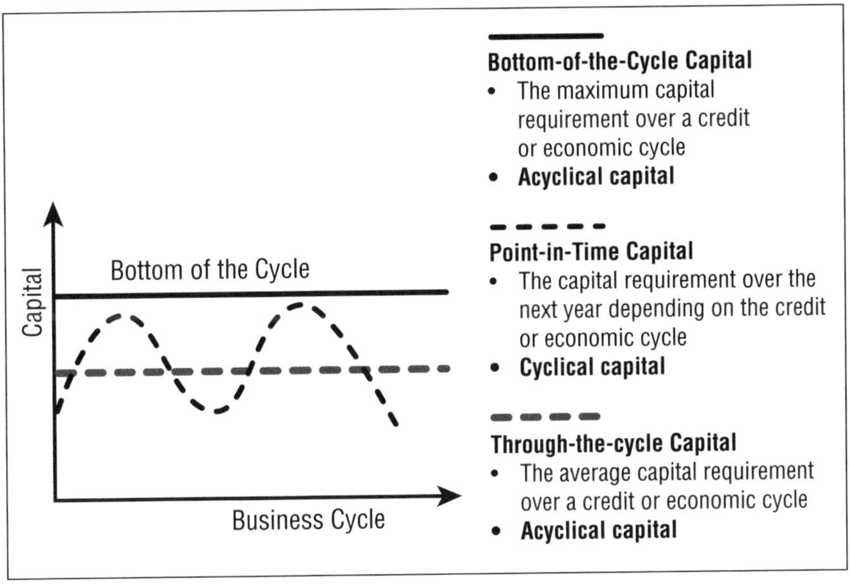

FIGURE 4.13 Capital Requirements Through-the-Cycle and Point-in-Time

The TTC models seek to ensure that a bank has sufficient capital levels throughout the average credit and business cycle. By extension, a bank should have sufficient levels of capital to withstand credit losses on average through the credit cycle, without substantially eroding its capital base. As a result, TTC models tend to require lower capital levels that may not be sufficient at times of stress when credit losses are accelerating and capital levels are eroding.

The PIT models seek to ensure that a bank has sufficient capital levels across all points in the credit and business cycle. By extension, a bank should have sufficient levels of capital available when credit losses are substantially eroding its capital base. As a result of this, PIT models tend to require higher capital levels.

The aim of the Basel Committee is to ensure that credit grades take cycles into account. Although PD estimates for most grading models are based on a one-year time horizon, many of the banks covered by Basel II will have loan portfolios that are not easily managed at any point in time, because they are comprised of illiquid loan assets that cannot be sold or securitized easily. The Accord requires banks to conduct scenario analysis on their IRB models to incorporate the impact that deteriorating economic conditions would have on PD estimates. The banks' final models should take these into account when granting (and thus grading) loans. Moreover, by requiring banks to average their PD estimates to establish a long-term average, the credit losses reflect TTC and not PIT, which may not be reliably quantified in advance given limited historical data to properly model the differences in loss experience over several cycles.

4.5.3 Calibrating Models: EL and UL

IRB models require the estimation of EL and UL. Over time a bank can estimate EL as the average loss incurred for specific loan portfolios, e.g., large corporates, personal credit cards, etc., on the basis of historical PD and LGD experience. EL represents the average amount a bank expects to lose from its loan portfolio over time and represents a cost of the bank's lending business. How reserves against EL are built up is an integral part of the bank's loan policy (See Chapter 1).

In practice, however, loan losses are unlikely to be uniform year on year, largely because of vagaries of the business cycle. Consequently, banks need to consider what losses they would incur during economic contractions in relation to losses they would incur during economic expansions. Losses in excess of EL are by nature—and definition—UL. These losses are estimated statistically, and it is highly unlikely that any bank would be able to predict such losses with total accuracy. If and when UL actually occur, the result would be a significant increase in loan loss provisions, which reduces a bank's income, and when a bank's income is insufficient to cover its losses, any deficit must be deducted from its capital. For this reason banks need to carry capital against UL.

Consequently, an additional model estimate of LGD should assume that a downturn in the economy will take place. Moreover, the Accord requires that capital be held to reflect the difference between the two LGD estimates, i.e., the estimate made in the projected downturn and the estimate made in the current circumstances. The different estimates of LGD will clearly vary across different classes of security and different lending portfolios.

4.5.4 The Usage Test

In addition to using grading models for calculating regulatory capital, any bank adopting either the Foundation or the Advanced IRB Approach must use the same models to make credit management decisions, and the bank must also transfer all significant asset classes to be managed based on the results derived from these approaches. Banks that are IRB compliant can only use the Standardized Approach to calculate regulatory capital on a small amount of their portfolios. This is particularly important for banks with operations in some jurisdictions where relevant information to properly design and implement either of the IRB Approaches may not be available.

4.5.5 Collateral in the IRB Approaches

The Basel II Accord offers three approaches by which collateral may reduce credit risk capital requirements. A bank can use any of the three approaches if it uses either the Standardized or the IRB Foundation Approach. If the bank adopts the Advanced IRB Approach then it must use one of two Comprehensive Approaches for the valuation and use of collateral. (See Section 4.3.3 above.)

Banks using the Advanced Comprehensive Approach can produce their own estimate of haircuts. There is also no restriction on the types of collateral, although banks must provide evidence of its value. Typically, banks value all investment-grade financial collateral by estimating the volatility of the value of the collateral instruments and the volatility of any applicable foreign exchange mismatches on a case-by-case basis. The Advanced Comprehensive Approach mirrors the Advanced IRB Approach for credit risk in that both quantitative and qualitative criteria must be met before it can be implemented. Further, Basel II permits banks to use a VaR model as an alternative to the Comprehensive approaches discussed above.

The quantitative and qualitative criteria for this VaR approach are the same as under the 1998 Market Risk Amendment.

4.6 Securitization

Previous chapters discussed securitization as a mechanism for reducing a bank's credit risk. The Basel Framework creates a specific set of rules for the supervision of securitization, applying to the originator of the assets that are securitized and to the bank holding the securitized assets as investments.

In a traditional securitization, the cash flow from an underlying pool of homogenous assets is used to pay interest and principal on at least two different tranches of a bond issued to finance the purchase of the homogenous asset pool. A tranche of a bond issue is effectively a separate bond in that each tranche will be subject to different terms for the payment of interest and principal. Consequently each tranche may have a different credit rating. They will however appear in the same documentation and will be secured by recourse to one underlying pool of assets.

A typical securitization may have a large nominal value of high-quality tranches, for example with AA ratings, and a number of smaller nominal value tranches some with very low grades, for example with a B rating, or which may be unrated. The lower-rated tranche, the junior tranche, will absorb losses before the higher-rated tranche, the senior tranche. These tranches are sold to investors. Payment of interest and principal depends on the performance of the underlying asset pool, as well as the claim on their performance set out in the terms and conditions.

4.6.1 Risk Transfer

From a regulatory perspective, one of the chief concerns is that the risk inherent in the securitized assets is not fully transferred to the bondholders, but is effectively retained by the originating bank. This implicit support essentially retains the credit risk on the bank's books. Moreover, originating banks have also subsidized first losses through such mechanisms as reducing their charges for servicing the securitized assets (paid by the investors) should defaults occur above a specified level. This effectively offsets (in part) any losses the investors would suffer when defaults occur.

For a bank that originates a securitization, capital relief under Basel II is contingent on the bank creating an effective and significant risk transfer from the originating bank to the investors in the bonds. The Accord does not specifically lay down parameters to quantify the "significant" risk transfer that allows for regulatory capital relief; the supervisory approach to securitization is flexible. This allows supervisors to react to innovations (in what is a rapidly developing market) more responsively, with principles-based regulation rather than regulation that is too prescriptive.

The origination requirements for supervisors to recognize a risk transfer by an originating bank are the same for both the Standardized and IRB Approaches. However, the risk weighting of the same tranche of a securitized bond could differ depending on the type of investor and/or banks that retain part of the securitization.

4.6.2 The Standardized Approach

Under the Standardized Approach, an investment in a tranche of a securitization is given the same risk weighting as the loan asset of an issuer with the same public-bond credit grade. Higher risk weights are applied for a tranche with an external rating below investment grade (Baa 3/BBB–). In addition, any unrated tranche held must be deducted directly from the capital of the bank; the deduction is split 50-50 between core and additional capital (basically Tier 1 and Tier 2). In contrast, unrated lending is weighted at 100%.

A deduction from capital, at the minimum 8% capital requirement, is effectively a risk weight of 1250%, the same effective cost (in capital terms) of a loan funded entirely by equity or 12.5 (= 100/8) times a normal 100% weighted loan, which consumes capital at 8%. This gives 12.5 × 100% = 1250% as the effective risk weight (this will be even higher if the bank's capital requirement is above the 8% minimum).

4.6.3 The IRB Approaches

Banks that use either the Foundation or the Advanced IRB Approach for calculating their credit risk capital requirement for the underlying assets must use the same approach for an investment in a securitization. However, in cases where the IRB Approach is not used for that underlying asset class, the IRB Approaches are replaced by three ways of calculating the capital requirement against holding an investment in a securitization exposure. These are:

- The Ratings-Based Approach (RBA)
- The Supervisory Formula Approach (SF)
- The Internal Assessment Approach (IAA)

The Ratings-Based Approach must be used if the securitization exposures are rated, or where a rating can be inferred from similar securitization issue. The RBA mirrors the Standardized Approach for calculating regulatory capital for loan assets. External public ratings (where they exist) of any securitization tranche must be used as the basis for calculating regulatory capital. However, the RBA uses a specific set of risk weights that calibrate the rating class more finely than the Standardized Approach does. This creates a greater number of risk-weight classes.

The RBA rating scale also takes into account the security of a tranche for payments and the number of assets covered by the securitization, i.e. the granularity, of the underlying assets. The scale gives preference, through the lower risk weights, to securitizations based on several assets, but penalizes concentration effects.

Importantly, the RBA does not make any distinction in risk weighting between an arm's length investor and an originator of the security when the originator continues to hold the tranche in securitized form as an investment. This way of holding securitizations is common in the US, where the ability to sell securitized tranches on short notice allows for the flexible management of a bank's credit portfolio as well as of its liquidity. Where an external or inferred rating cannot be used, either the Supervisory Formula or the Internal Assessment Approach must be applied.

The Supervisory Formula (and the Internal Assessment Approach) may be applied to unrated tranches just as in the IRB Approaches to loan assets. The SF seeks to establish the equivalent IRB capital charge of a tranche had the exposure not been securitized. This capital charge at tranche level is known as the K_{IRB}. The sum of all the K_{IRB} of every tranche of a securitization should add up to the same capital charge as the exposures would have if they had remained on the balance sheet. The K_{IRB} may be calculated on an aggregate portfolio basis for the assets subject to the securitization. In this respect it differs from the IRB Approach to underlying loan assets, where the assets must be assessed individually for their capital charge.

The Internal Assessment Approach has very limited application and can only be used with the approval of the appropriate national supervisor because it is primarily designed to deal with asset-backed commercial paper programs, which are commonly used in the US market to securitize such assets as credit card receivables. To use the IAA a bank must employ the same methodology as a recognized rating agency to create each internal assessment of the risk grading of a tranche of a securitization. The bank can then "map" its ratings to the rating scale published by the rating agency. The risk weight of its exposures is generated in the same way as under the RBA.

4.6.4 Basel III Securitization Framework

In the aftermath of the global financial crisis, the Basel II framework for securitization was found to have several shortcomings, not least a mechanistic reliance on external ratings and a poorly calibrated risk-weighting formula. In its update in Basel III, the committee has sought to make the securitization framework more risk sensitive, more prudently calibrated, broadly consistent with the underlying framework for credit risk, and simpler: there are fewer approaches and exceptional treatments. Basel III's securitization framework forms part of the Basel III agenda to reform banking regulatory standards in response to the global financial crisis. It will come into effect in January 2018.

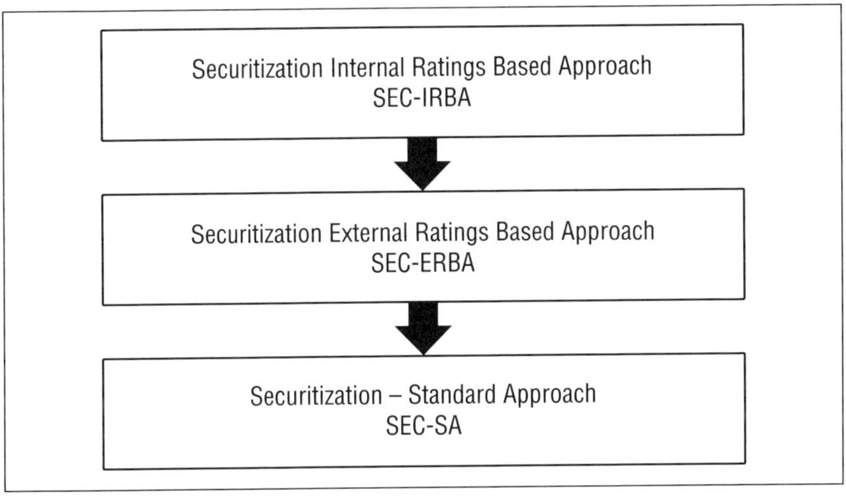

FIGURE 4.14 Basel III Securitization Framework
Source: Basel Committee on Banking Supervision, Basel III Document, Revisions to the Securitization Framework, December 11, 2014

In contrast to Basel II, the Basel III framework is simpler; the hierarchy of use is shown in Figure 4.14 SEC-IRBA is the top of the revised hierarchy. In order to use SEC-IRBA, a bank should use a supervisor-approved model for the underlying exposures in the securitization and have sufficient information to calculate K_{IRB} (i.e., the capital charge for the underlying exposures utilizing the IRB framework). If a bank cannot use SEC-IRBA, it must use SEC-ERBA unless reliance on external ratings is not permitted in its jurisdiction or a securitization is unrated. If a bank cannot use either

SEC-IRBA or SEC-ERBA, it must use SEC-SA, which is generally a more conservative calibration.

Securitization Internal Ratings Based Approach (SEC-IRBA)
SEC-IRBA is the first step in the revised hierarchy. The underlying model is the Simplified Supervisory Formula Approach which uses K_{IRB} as a key input. As noted in Section 4.6.3, K_{IRB} is the capital charge at tranche level. Another shortcoming of Basel II is that it ignores the effects of maturity. The SFA only looks at the risk of default over a one-year horizon and therefore ignores the risk of possible deterioration thereafter. In response to this, SEC-IRBA incorporates tranche maturity as an additional risk factor.

Securitization External Ratings Based Approach (SEC-ERBA)
As noted in Section 4.6.3, Basel II's RBA methodology assigns risk weights according to the external rating of the exposure, the seniority, and the granularity of the underlying pool. Basel III has determined that it is necessary to consider some additional risk factors: tranche thickness of non-senior tranches, the size of the tranche compared to the entire transaction; and tranche maturity. To avoid overstating the effects of maturity, the risk weights for longer-maturity tranches are reduced. Finally, the committee found that credit rating agencies already incorporate granularity in their ratings of a particular tranche and therefore Basel III does not require a granularity adjustment when external ratings are used.

Securitization Standardized Approach (SEC-SA)
A bank that cannot use either SEC-IRBA or SEC-ERBA must use SEC-SA instead. This is a generally more conservative calibration and uses K_{SA} as the model input where K_{SA} is the capital charge for the underlying exposures using the Standardized Approach for credit risk.

Under Basel III, a slightly modified, and more conservative SEC-SA is the only approach available for re-securitizations.

In general a bank that cannot use any of the three outlined approaches for a given securitization exposure would assign the exposure a risk weight of 1,250%.

4.7 Regulatory Guidance on Leveraged Lending

In March 2013, the Office of the Comptroller of the Currency (OCC), the Board of Governors of the Federal Reserve System (the Fed) and the Federal Deposit Insurance Corporation (FDIC), together "the US agencies," issued joint guidance on leveraged lending for financial institutions. In November 2014, the US agencies released findings of their Shared National Credit Review and also released a Frequently Asked Questions (FAQ) document to supplement the March 2013 document.

According to Dealogic Ltd., the volume of global leveraged finance (leveraged loans and high-yield bonds) totaled USD 2.1 trillion in 2014. Leveraged loans in the US alone totaled US 1.09 trillion in 2014. The leveraged finance market has benefited from investor demand for higher yielding securities (both bonds and loans) given the backdrop of historically low interest rates in the US and Europe. However, the US agencies cautioned in their 2013 guidance that growth in investor demand has also been accompanied by more aggressive capital structures, less onerous repayment schedules, and more lenient covenant or collateral requirements

The credit risks to financial institutions that originate and participate in such transactions may be amplified in times of market stress when investor demand for such securities suddenly falls away. As a result, the US agencies updated their previous guidance from 2001 so as to ensure sound lending practices for leveraged finance activities. According to the guidance, institutions that do not comply with the guidance "will be subject to criticism" and "an institution unwilling or unable to implement strong risk management processes will incur significant risks and should cease their participation in this type of lending until their processes improve significantly."

The guidance applies to all institutions regulated by the US agencies; for US banking institutions the guidance applies on an enterprise-wide basis. For foreign institutions with US charters the guidance applies to all leveraged loans originated and distributed in the US. It may transpire that regulators in other countries may look to the US guidance as a model for new policy introductions.

4.7.1 Defining Leveraged Finance

The term leveraged finance is very broad and encompasses a wide array of activities. However, most definitions include some of the following:

- Finance for private equity-led transactions such as leveraged buyouts, acquisitions, dividend distributions, or recapitalizations
- Highly leveraged transactions, i.e., where the borrower's total debt/EBITDA or senior debt/EBITDA exceeds 4.0x or 3.0x, respectively, or other levels appropriate to the specific industry or market

- Transactions where the borrower is recognized in the capital markets as highly leveraged
- Transactions where, after financing, the borrower's leverage ratios significantly exceed industry norms or its own historical levels

4.7.2 Minimum Requirements in Loan Policies and Procedures

Section 1.2 described the importance to credit risk management of a well-crafted loan policy. For those institutions involved, either as underwriters or participants, in leveraged lending, the US agencies outlined their minimum expectations on the following topics to be covered in policies and procedures.

- Definition of Leveraged Lending
- General Policy Expectations
- Participations Purchased
- Underwriting Standards
- Valuation Standards
- Pipeline Management
- Reporting and Analytics
- Risk Rating Leveraged Loans
- Credit Analysis
- Problem Credit Management
- Deal Sponsors
- Credit Review
- Stress Testing
- Conflicts of Interest
- Reputational Risk
- Compliance

4.7.3 Summary of US Regulatory Guidance for Leveraged Finance

To summarize, a financial institution is expected to maintain:

- Safe-and-sound loan structures: appropriate capital structure, sound business premise, reasonable cash flow, and balance sheet leverage which, combined with supportable forecasts, clearly support a borrower's capacity to repay and de-lever within a reasonable period
- A definition of leveraged lending that is consistently applied across all business lines

- Underwriting standards that define acceptable leverage levels and amortization expectations
- A framework for credit limits and concentration that is consistent with the institution's risk appetite
- Sound procedures that enable bank management to identify, aggregate, and monitor leveraged exposures and comply with credit policy across all business lines
- Policies and procedures regarding deal pipeline that provides real-time information on exposures, limits, and any exceptions to timings of expected distributions or approved hold levels
- Guidelines regarding periodic portfolio and pipeline stress tests to quantify the impact of economic and market conditions on the institution's asset quality, earnings, liquidity, and capital

In times of market disruption such as after the Lehman Brothers' failure in the US, the importance of including pipeline transactions is key.

Furthermore, financial institutions should also be mindful of other risks such as reputational risks associated with poorly underwritten transactions which may have wider ramifications or exacerbate systemic risk within an economy. See *Operational Risk Management*, another title in the GARP Financial Risk and Regulation Series for a more thorough discussion of reputational risks.

4.8 Summary

This chapter has addressed the regulatory treatment of credit risk as outlined in the Basel Accords.

Linking capital and credit risk

- Risk-based capital regulation focuses on establishing a direct relationship between a bank's risks and its equity and capital to ensure that banks operate safely, soundly, and prudently.
- Banking regulation builds on establishing regulatory capital levels that reflect the inherent riskiness of the various assets the bank owns.

The Evolution of the Basel Accords

- International banking regulatory cooperation is conducted through the Basel Committee on Banking Supervision (BCBS).

- The Basel Committee formulates broad banking supervisory standards, such as the Basel Accords, and develops guidelines for both banks and regulators.
- Basel I linked risk-based capital requirements to the credit risks banks take, where credit risk was measured using a grid of risk weights. These risk weights change nominal asset values into risk-weighted asset (RWA) values for calculating regulatory capital.
- Basel I had several shortcomings, such as a narrow focus on credit risk, no connection between credit risk and maturity, no difference across various gradations of credit risk, no consideration of correlation and no recognition of risk reduction effects or tools. These shortcomings limited its application and initially led to changes and extensions to the Accord, and eventually to Basel II.
- Basel II consists of three interrelated pillars:
  - Pillar 1 sets minimum capital requirements to reflect credit risk, market risk, and operational risk, and offers banks three different alternatives of varying complexity to calculate their minimum regulatory capital requirements.
  - Pillar 2 complements and strengthens Pillar 1 by establishing a prudential supervision process.
  - Pillar 3 outlines the effective use of market discipline as a lever to strengthen disclosure and encourage sound banking practices.
- Basel III was designed in the aftermath of the global financial crisis. The overriding objective of Basel III was to reduce the likelihood that such a devastating crisis could reoccur in the future.
- A series of documents, amendments, and agreements amend and update Basel II and collectively form Basel III. The Basel III framework is to be implemented incrementally and should be fully in place by the end of 2018.
- Unlike Basel I and II, which were micro-prudential, Basel III has macro-prudential features, i.e., it has a focus on the stability of the financial system as a whole.
- Basel III increases capital requirements for individual banks, focusing on the ability to survive stress periods. It also includes new liquidity rules as well as introducing non-risk-based leverage requirements.

Credit risk: Standardized Approach

- Under Basel II, the Standardized Approach provides differential risk weights for corporate, sovereign, and bank exposures depending on how the exposures are assessed by external agencies such as OECD export credit agencies or credit rating agencies.

- The public rating of debt in the international markets is dominated by three credit rating agencies: Moody's Investors Service, Standard & Poor's, and Fitch Ratings.
- Basel II applies six criteria to an External Credit Assessment Institution (ECAI), a rating agency, to test if it meets the necessary requirements for its ratings to be used by banks as part of their capital calculations.
- If a credit is not rated by either an OECD export credit agency or a credit rating agency such as Moody's, S&P, or Fitch, Basel II mandates a 100% credit risk weighting.
- The ratings of bonds issued by the same issuer can differ because of factors such as legal covenants, undertakings, and even the security backing them. These features are themselves subject to rules and regulations and may bring into question the appropriateness of the grade assigned to a company's unsecured credit standing.
- Basel II sets out specific rules for risk-weighting of various assets:
  - Claims on sovereign entities are subject to the discretion of the national supervisor and can be set as low as 0% regardless of the sovereign's rating.
  - Two approaches for grading the risk weighting of a bank: Option 1 requires banks to be rated one notch below the sovereign, and Option 2 allows the risk weighting to reflect the external rating of the bank. An unrated bank would carry a 100% risk weighting.
  - Retail and SME exposures are weighted at 75% provided they are included in a retail portfolio.
  - Lending against residential property carries a risk weighting of 35% as long as the loan is secured on property owned and occupied or rented out to others by the borrower.
  - Counterparties rated B– or lower carry a 150% risk weighting but the risk weight may be reduced to 100% or lower if a specific provision has been allocated to the obligation.

Credit risk: Internal Ratings Based Approaches

- The Internal Ratings Based (IRB) Approach builds on the concept that capital requirements should reflect unexpected losses (UL), as expected losses (EL) are already priced in and adequate provisions made in a bank's financial statements.
- The IRB Approaches are based on the assumption that the value of a loan on a bank's balance sheet and the risk of the loan that the bank

assumes depends on 1) systematic risk, reflecting, for example, economic or credit cycles that impact all exposures similarly; and 2) idiosyncratic risk, those factors that are credit – or facility-specific and only impact that particular exposure.

- The parameters of the IRB Approach are known as the risk components and are the probability of default (PD), loss given default (LGD), exposure at default (EAD), effective maturity of the loan (M), and size factors (S) for corporate exposures.
- PD depends on the relationship between the likelihood that the systematic factor impacts the value of the assets so that there is a default.
- Assuming various degrees of correlation, the PD can be quantified, and based on this input EL can be measured and UL can be inferred.
- The IRB Approach comprises two methodologies: Foundation IRB Approach and Advanced IRB Approach. The difference between these approaches relates to the degree to which banks estimate the risk parameters of their grading models.
- In the Foundation IRB Approach:
  - A bank's credit model estimates only the PD of the borrower based on a minimum requirement of five years of financial data.
  - LGD and EAD are set by the national supervisor and will depend on the asset classes and collateral held by the bank. M is set at 2½ years albeit at the discretion of the national supervisor.
  - Adjustments for collateral may be made.
- In the Advanced IRB Approach:
  - A bank must estimate all the risk components—PD, LGD, and EAD—for all asset classes.
  - Maturity and size factors do not require estimation. For corporate exposures other than to large corporates, national supervisors may allow a uniform 2½-year assumption for M. For corporate exposures to large corporates, M must be specific to the loan.
  - For retail exposures, the IRB Approach offers only the Advanced Approach, therefore a bank must provide its own estimate of PD, LGD, and EAD. However, these are not based on individual exposures but on pools of similar exposures. A bank that is not using the IRB Approach will use the Standardized Approach with respect to retail exposures.

Other considerations

- All grading models have the ability to estimate a greater or lesser number of grades with accuracy, thus discriminating between the quality of different borrowers.
- The ability of a grading model to accurately predict the PD of a counterparty can only be judged by looking at past data to assess how accurate model predictions have been.
- The "through-the-cycle" credit grading models attempt to estimate the probability of loss taking "normal" credit cycles into account.
- The "point-in-time" credit grading models attempt to grade credits based on the current state of the economy.
- Basel II requires banks to run scenarios on their IRB models that allow for deterioration in economic conditions, and to take these into account when granting (and thus grading) loans.
- A bank can estimate over time the average or expected loss it could incur for specific loan portfolios, e.g., large corporates, personal credit cards, etc., on the basis of historical default (PD) and historical losses (LGD).
- A bank needs to consider what losses it would incur in a "bad" year. The level of these losses is known as the unexpected loss.
- If unexpected losses actually occur, the result would be a significant increase in provisions that would be deducted from the bank's income.
- If a bank's income is insufficient to cover such losses any deficit must be deducted from its capital.
- An additional model estimate of loss given default should assume that a downturn in the economy would take place.
- Basel II requires capital to be held to reflect the difference between the two LGD estimates: an estimate made in the projected downturn and an estimate made in the current circumstances.
- A bank must transfer all significant asset classes to either the Foundation or the Advanced IRB Approach, and can only use the Standardized Approach to calculate regulatory capital on a small amount of its portfolio.

Collateral

- Collateral is defined as assets pledged by a borrower to secure a loan or other credit, and which are subject to seizure in the event of default.
- Under Basel II there is recognition of both financial as well as physical assets and receivables as collateral.

- A reduction in the value of collateral over its market value is termed a haircut.
- The three techniques for reducing credit risk capital due to the presence of collateral are: the Simple Approach, the Comprehensive Approach, and the Advanced Comprehensive Approach.
- The credit quality of the counterparty and the value of the collateral must not be closely related to one another.
- A bank may use the Simple or either of the Comprehensive approaches to collateral in their banking book, but not both.
- Under the Simple Approach the risk weight of the instrument, which is collateralizing or partly collateralizing the exposure, is substituted for the risk weight of the counterparty.
- Under the Comprehensive Approach, financial collateral includes additional instruments to those included in the Simple Approach.
- Under the Comprehensive Approach, standard collateral "haircuts" reduce the value of the collateral that can then be offset against the underlying exposure.
- A bank using the Advanced Comprehensive Approach can produce its own estimate of haircuts. There is also no restriction on the types of collateral although a bank must provide evidence of its value.
- Non-financial collateral includes real estate, receivables, and other collateral allowed at the local supervisor's discretion.
- Basel II permits a bank to use a VaR model as an alternative to the Comprehensive approaches in valuing collateral.

Securitization

- Securitization distributes risk from assets in a homogenous pool by issuing new securities backed by these assets and their cash flows.
- These securities are sold to investors who share the risk and reward from those assets.
- Each tranche is subject to different terms for the payment of interest and principal and as a consequence may have a different credit rating. The expectation is that a lower-rated tranche, the junior tranche, will absorb losses prior to that of the higher-rated tranche, the senior tranche.
- One of the major concerns of supervisors with respect to securitization is that the risk inherent in the securitized assets is not fully transferred to the bondholders, but is retained by the originating bank. This is known as implicit support.

- The origination requirements for supervisors to recognize a risk transfer by an originating bank are the same for both the Standardized and IRB Approaches.
- Under the Standardized Approach an investment in a tranche of a securitization is given the same risk weighting as the loan asset of an issuer with the same public bond credit grade.
- A capital deduction is the same as the effective cost, in capital terms, of a loan funded entirely by equity.
- Banks that use either the Foundation or the Advanced IRB Approach for calculating their credit risk capital requirement for the underlying assets must use the same approach for an investment in a securitization.
- To use the Internal Assessment Approach a bank must employ the same methodology as a recognized rating agency to create each internal assessment of the risk grading of a securitization tranche.
- In the aftermath of the global financial crisis, Basel II's securitization framework was found to have several shortcomings, not least an over-reliance on external ratings and a poorly calibrated risk-weighting formula.
  - Basel III's securitization framework is simpler and is broadly consistent with the underlying framework for credit risk.
  - Basel III's securitization framework consists of a hierarchy of three levels.
  - Securitization Internal Ratings Based Approach (SEC-IRBA). In order to use this approach, a bank should use a supervisor-approved model for the underlying exposures in the securitization and demonstrate it has sufficient information to calculate K_{IRB}, the capital charge for the underlying exposures utilizing the IRB framework.
  - Securitization External Ratings Based Approach (SEC-ERBA). If a bank cannot use SEC-IRBA, it must use SEC-ERBA unless reliance on external ratings is not permitted in its jurisdiction or a securitization is unrated.
  - Securitization Standard Approach (SEC-SA). If a bank cannot use either SEC-IRBA or SEC-ERBA, it must use SEC-SA, which is generally a more conservative calibration.
- Under Basel III, a slightly modified and more conservative version of SEC-SA is the only approach available for re-securitizations.
- In general a bank that cannot use any of the three outlined approaches for a given securitization exposure would assign the exposure a risk weight of 1,250%.

A Note on Leveraged Lending

- In the US, the Fed, OCC, and FDIC have jointly issued guidance on leveraged lending. The purpose of this is to ensure sound lending practice for leveraged finance activities.
- The credit risks to financial institutions that originate and participate in highly leveraged transactions may be amplified in times of market stress when investor demand for such securities suddenly falls away.
- The guidance requires that a financial institution involved in leveraged lending, either as an originator or a participant, needs to demonstrate the following:
    - Safe-and-sound loan structures which clearly support a borrower's capacity to repay and de-lever within a reasonable period
    - A definition of leveraged lending that is consistently applied across all business lines
    - Underwriting standards that define acceptable leverage levels and amortization expectations
    - A framework for credit limits and concentration that is consistent with the institution's risk appetite
    - Sound procedures that enable banks' management to identify, aggregate, and monitor leveraged exposures and comply with credit policy across all business lines
    - Policies and procedures regarding deal pipelines that provide real-time information on exposures, limits, and any exceptions to timings of expected distributions or approved hold levels
    - Guidelines regarding periodic portfolio and pipeline stress tests to quantify the impact of economic and market conditions on the institution's asset quality, earnings, liquidity, and capital

Glossary

Advanced Internal Ratings Based Approach The Advanced Internal Ratings Based Approach refers to a set of credit risk measurement techniques and capital adequacy rules outlined in the Basel II Accord that allows banks to develop their own empirical models, requiring them to calculate most inputs, to quantify their required capital.

Asset Backed Security (ABS) An Asset Backed Security is a financial instrument backed by pools of loans or other types of securitizable cash-flow-generating assets and is sold to investors who then receive payments based on the cash flows generated by the assets in the underlying pool.

Asset-based loan Asset-based loans allow the borrower to pledge a specific asset or combination of assets, such as inventory, machinery or equipment, as collateral to cover a loan.

Asset Management Company (AMC) An Asset Management Company is an entity tasked with managing assets on behalf of a principal. In banking and credit risk management, it typically refers to a so-called "bad bank" that has a long-term mandate and manages non-performing loans and assets to maximize the ultimate recovery value on behalf of a bank.

Bank A bank is a financial intermediary that takes deposits, makes loans, arranges payments, holds a banking license, and is subject to regulatory supervision by a banking regulator.

Banking book The banking book of a bank is the portfolio of assets, primarily loans, that a bank expects to hold until maturity. It typically refers to the loans the bank underwrites.

Basel Accords The Basel Accords (Basel I, II, the Market Risk Amendment, and Basel III) are the cornerstones of international risk-based banking regulation and are the results of a collaborative attempt by banking regulators from major economies to create a globally valid and widely applicable framework for banks and bank risk management.

Basel Committee on Banking Supervision The Basel Committee on Banking Supervision (BCBS) is a forum for regulatory cooperation on banking supervision issues. It was established by central bank governors, and consists of senior representatives from bank supervisory authorities and central banks from major economies.

Bond A bond is a legally binding contract through which the borrower, the issuer of the bond, borrows the principal, an amount specified in the bond, from an investor and in exchange pays a specified amount of interest, referred to as the coupon payment, usually at regular intervals, and at maturity repays the principal.

Borrower A borrower receives money by borrowing money with the promise to repay the amount borrowed, the principal, and to pay compensation for borrowing the funds, interest, to the lender.

Capital adequacy Capital adequacy is achieved when a bank's capital ratio meets or exceeds the minimum capital ratio set by the Basel Accords or by its national banking regulator.

Capital requirement Capital requirement determines the minimum capital levels regulators require each bank to hold against its risk levels.

Capital Capital denotes financial assets or the financial value of assets, such as cash, or the long-term financial contribution of investors in a corporation.

Cash flow loan A cash flow loan provides funds that are repaid from the cash flow generated by the borrower's operations.

Central bank A central bank is the principal monetary authority of a country, or a group of countries. It may also exercise regulatory and supervisory responsibilities over other banks, arrange payments between banks and, when needed, provide stability to the financial and banking system.

Clearinghouse A clearinghouse guarantees the financial performance of a trade on an exchange by becoming the buyer to each seller and seller to each buyer, and provides clearing and settlement services for financial transactions.

Collateral Collateral is an asset pledged by a borrower to secure a loan or other credit and is forfeited to the lender in the event of the borrower's default.

Collateralized Debt Obligation (CDO) A Collateralized Debt Obligation (CDO) is a type of structured asset-backed security. Its value is determined by payments derived from a specific portfolio of fixed-income generating assets or instruments.

Commercial paper Commercial paper is an unsecured, short-term debt security typically issued by a large, financially strong, organization that uses the proceeds to finance its operations.

Committed facility A committed facility is a type of loan, whereby the terms and conditions, such as margins, fees, and duration, are clearly defined in a formal agreement by the bank and are imposed on the borrower. So long as the borrower is in compliance with the terms and conditions of the facility, the bank is obliged to provide the funding.

Common risk factors Common risk factors are risk factors that may impact several obligors with similar exposures, financial instruments, or financial assets in the same way at the same time.

Consortium A consortium denotes a combined underwriting of loans by a select group of banks, also called a syndicate.

Corporate bonds A corporate bond is issued by a corporation to raise money from investors, and in return the investors receive interest payments from the corporation issuing the bonds.

Corporate credit risk Corporate credit risk is the risk of loss resulting from the non-payment of a corporate financial instrument.

Correlation Correlation is a single measure of association between two variables, establishes the strength of a statistical relationship, and also forms the basis for statistical regression.

Cost of credit The cost of credit is the interest rate, required return, or other compensation associated with securing and using credit.

Cost of funds The cost of funds is the interest rate, required return, or other compensation associated with securing and using capital.

Counterparty A counterparty is a party to a contract who is contractually bound and is expected to perform—deliver securities, make payments, etc.—sometime in the future.

Counterparty credit risk Counterparty credit risk is the risk that the other party to a contract or agreement will fail to perform under the terms of the agreement; it is particularly relevant for trading.

Covariance Covariance is a measure of association between two variables that quantifies the change between these variables.

Covenant A covenant is an agreement that requires one party to do, or refrain from doing, specified actions and is imposed on the borrower by a lender to prevent a potential deterioration in the borrower's financial and business condition.

Credit analysis Credit analysis is a structured approach to analyze, assess, and evaluate the creditworthiness of a business, organization, or an individual credit or similar exposure.

Credit concentration risk Credit concentration risk is the risk stemming from a single large exposure or group of exposures that are adversely impacted by similar variations in conditions, events, or circumstances.

Credit Default Swap (CDS) A credit default swap is a swap where the protection buyer makes a series of payments to the protection seller, and the protection seller provides a payment if a financial instrument, such as a bond or a loan, or a portfolio of financial instruments experiences a predefined credit event.

Credit derivative **A credit derivative is a contract that allows the use of a derivative instrument to transfer credit risk from one party to another. It provides protection if a credit instrument, such as a bond or loan, or portfolio of credit instruments experiences a credit event.**

Credit event A credit event can be a default on a loan or similar exposure, or delays making full or partial interest and/or principal payments. It may also include the impact of a downgrade of an external credit rating.

Credit grading model A credit grading or rating model quantifies the relative creditworthiness of a borrower, exposure, or facility.

Credit portfolio model A credit portfolio model is a computational system used to quantify the credit risk and creditworthiness of borrowers, exposures, or facilities and computes both expected and unexpected losses.

Credit portfolio risk Credit portfolio risk is the potential loss a bank can suffer from default, or delayed or missed repayment or interest payments, or a credit quality/rating downgrade in its credit portfolio.

Credit quality Credit quality reflects the risk associated with a loan, borrower, or facility. A higher credit quality translates to a higher credit grade or credit rating.

Credit rating A credit rating identifies the relative creditworthiness of a borrower, exposure, or facility by assigning a credit grade.

Credit rating agency (CRA) A credit rating agency evaluates the creditworthiness of various borrowers, issuers, or credits.

Credit risk Credit risk is the risk of loss due to non-payment of interest or non-repayment of a loan, bond, or other credit facility.

Credit risk management Credit risk management is a structured approach to monitoring, measuring, and managing exposures to reduce the risk of potential loss due to default.

Credit risk mitigation techniques A credit risk mitigation technique reduces credit risk through the use of collateral, loan guarantees, securitization, or insurance.

Credit score A credit score is a quantitative indicator of the relative creditworthiness of a borrower compared to a larger pool of borrowers, and is used as an indicator of the relative chance of default of that borrower.

Credit spread A credit spread is the yield differential between different securities caused by differences in their credit quality.

Credit VaR(CVaR) Credit Value-at-Risk is a quantitative estimate of the credit risk of the portfolio and is typically the difference between expected and unexpected losses on a credit portfolio over a one-year time horizon expressed at a certain statistical confidence level.

Default Default is the failure to pay interest or principal according to contractual terms and occurs when a debtor or counterparty is unable or unwilling to make a timely payment or delivery.

Default risk Default risk is the potential loss due to default.

Derivative A (financial) derivative does not have an intrinsic value of its own, rather its value changes in response to changes in the value of a related underlying financial asset or commodity, and includes swaps, options, forwards, and futures.

Disclosure Disclosure is the dissemination of otherwise internal information about the conditions, operations, and plans of an organization that allows for a proper and transparent evaluation of that organization.

Economic capital Economic capital is the amount of capital a bank needs in the case of loss events. It covers all risks across a bank and is essential for a bank to survive in the long-term.

Equity Equity is the capital raised from shareholders and from retained earnings, and reflects the ownership interest in a corporation.

Exchange A (financial) exchange is a formal, organized, physical or electronic marketplace where trades between investors follow standardized procedures.

Expected Loss (EL) Expected loss describes the amount of losses that can be expected to occur.

Export Credit Agency (ECA) An Export Credit Agency is a private or quasi-governmental institution that acts as an intermediary between national governments and exporters to issue export financing.

Exposure at Default (EAD) Exposure at Default is the maximum loss the lender or counterparty may suffer in case of a default.

External Credit Assessment Institutions (ECAI) External Credit Assessment Institutions provide credit assessments that banking regulators allow banks to use in computing their regulatory capital requirements.

Fair market price Fair market price is the price an asset would fetch if sold on the market to a willing buyer.

Financial asset A financial asset derives its value from a specific contractual claim and typically includes bonds, loans, stocks, money, currency, derivatives, certain commodities, and other assets of value.

Financial instrument A financial instrument is a representation of an ownership interest claim or the contractual or contingent claim to receive or deliver cash, another financial instrument, or an asset, and can either be a cash instrument, e.g., cash, securities, loans, bonds, notes, or equity, or a derivative instrument, e.g., forward, future, option, or swap.

Fixed income instrument A fixed income instrument, such as a bond, provides fixed and known periodic interest payments and the repayment of the principal at maturity.

Fixed interest rate A fixed interest rate is an interest rate that does not change over the life of a loan, bond, or other form of credit.

Fixed-interest-rate loan A fixed-interest-rate loan is a loan where the contractual interest rate that determines the periodic interest rate payments does not change during the lifetime of the loan.

Floating-rate loan A floating-rate loan is a loan where the interest rate on the loan is tied to an underlying index or base rate and, as a result, may change during the life of the loan.

Foundation IRB Approach The Foundation IRB Approach refers to a set of credit risk measurement techniques and capital adequacy rules outlined in the Basel II Accord. Under this approach, a bank develops its own empirical models to quantify the probability-of-default estimate required to calculate its capital for credit risk.

Governance Governance relates to the rules, processes, policies, and regulations outlining and defining the capacity, operational management, and administration of an organization, business, or other entity.

Hedging Hedging reduces risk by matching a position as closely as possible with an opposite and offsetting position in a financial instrument that tracks or mirrors the value changes in the position.

Historical frequency model A historical frequency model quantifies credit risk and other risk exposures based on empirical and historical realizations of credit risk events.

Idiosyncratic risk Idiosyncratic risk represents risks that are particular to the conditions and circumstances of one or a defined group of individual borrowers, assets. or securities.

Insolvency Insolvency occurs when liabilities exceed assets. While not synonymous with bankruptcy or illiquidity, it typically leads to either or both.

Interest rate An interest rate is the price of credit and is the rate charged for accessing and using borrowed funds.

Interest rate margin The interest rate margin is the difference between the interest income a bank earns on its assets and the interest expense it pays on its liabilities.

Interest rate risk Interest rate risk is the potential loss of value due to the variability of interest rates.

Interest rate risk in the banking book The interest rate risk in the banking book is caused by maturity differences between bank assets and liabilities, by differing interest rates used for pricing, and by differing repricing points.

Internal Assessment Approach (IAA) The Internal Assessment Approach allows a bank to map its internal credit assessment of a securitization exposure to an equivalent external credit rating from a nationally recognized statistical rating organization.

Internal Ratings Based (IRB) Approach The Internal Ratings Based Approach allows a bank, after being granted permission from its national regulator, to use its own estimates to determine its regulatory minimum capital requirement for credit risk.

Investment bank An investment bank predominantly deals with corporate and institutional customers, issues financial securities in the financial and capital markets, provides advice on transactions such as mergers and acquisitions, manages investments and trades on its own account.

Junior debt Junior debt is subordinated to more senior debt in case of bankruptcy, default, or similar events, but has priority before equity.

Lending guideline A lending guideline typically includes financial performance standards, collateral requirement standards, and possibly loan repricing standards to better link exposures to risks and pricing.

Letter of credit A letter of credit guarantees payment by a bank on behalf of its customer who pays a fee to the bank for providing the guarantee.

Leverage Leverage reflects the amount or proportion of debt used in the financing structure of an organization. The higher the leverage, the more debt the company is using.

LIBOR (London Interbank Offered Rate) LIBOR, London Interbank Offered Rate, is a daily reference rate based on the average interest rate banks in London charge other banks, on the other side of the transaction, when borrowing and lending.

Line of credit A line of credit is an uncommitted credit facility that establishes the maximum amount of funds a financial institution will advance to a borrower.

Loan loss reserve A loan loss reserve or "allowance for loan losses" or a "credit loss reserve" is the portion of loans set aside to absorb anticipated loan losses.

Loan policy The loan policy outlines a bank's credit strategy, the principles of its lending practices, the responsibility of its relationship managers, compliance requirements, the loan and other credit products the bank may offer, and those that it may not offer.

Loan portfolio A loan portfolio contains all the loans, leases, and other credits a bank has either underwritten directly or participates in.

Loan review A loan review is an independent evaluation of compliance with loan, credit, and underwriting policies and assures compliance with credit standards and banking regulations. It is typically carried out by a bank's auditors on behalf of the senior loan committee, senior management, or the board of directors.

Long position A long position, the opposite of a short position, represents the ownership position of an asset. When the asset's value increases, the position's value increases and when the asset's value decreases, the position's value decreases.

Long-term lending Long-term lending is often considered to have a maturity exceeding 15 years, though some banks and countries may use a shorter period to describe long-term lending. Long-term lending finances major capital projects or expenditures.

Loss Given Default (LGD) Loss Given Default is the actual loss suffered in the wake of a default. It is a function of the recovery rate and the exposure at default.

Market risk Market risk is defined as the risk of losses in on- and off-balance-sheet positions arising from movements in market prices, and typically encompasses the risks pertaining to interest-rate related instruments and equities in the trading book, and foreign exchange risk and commodities risk throughout the bank.

Market risk capital Market risk capital is capital allocated against possible market losses.

Maturity Maturity is the time period until a loan, bond, or other credit is repaid fully.

Medium-term lending Medium-term lending generally has a maturity not exceeding three or five years and finances ongoing investments in machinery, equipment, facilities, or cyclical needs.

Monetary policy Monetary policy is the process by which the monetary authority of a country controls the supply of money, often targeting a rate of interest. Monetary policy is usually used to attain a set of objectives oriented towards the economic growth and stability of a country.

Mortgage A mortgage finances the purchase of real estate that is pledged as collateral for the loan.

Off-balance-sheet activity An off-balance-sheet activity is not recorded on the balance sheet and can include assets, debt, or financing-related activities such as derivatives, loan commitments, or other contingent exposures that could pose a risk to a bank.

Over-the-counter (OTC) market The over-the-counter market is a decentralized market without a physical marketplace, where both standardized and non-standardized securities and other financial instruments are traded.

Paid-in-capital Paid-in-capital is the (equity) capital that the owners have invested in a corporation.

Permanent financing Permanent financing provides capital either through equity or long-term debt to purchase, develop, and operate long-term fixed assets such as factories, equipment, and machinery.

Pillars of the Basel II Accord The Basel II Accord consists of three pillars. Pillar 1 focuses on minimum capital requirements for the three major risks bank face credit risk, operational risk, and market risk; Pillar 2 focuses on supervisory review and processes for capital adequacy; and Pillar 3 focuses on market discipline and transparency.

Point-in-Time (PIT) capital model Point-in-Time capital models determine regulatory capital adequacy to reflect the risk and the associated regulatory capital requirements, at a specific point in time.

Potential Future Exposure (PFE) Potential future exposure quantifies counterparty credit risk by evaluating existing trades, positions, and other exposures in light of possible future variability in market prices, rates, or yields during their likely lifetime.

Price of credit The price of credit is the rate charged for accessing and using borrowed funds.

Prime lending rate The prime lending rate or prime rate is the rate the banks typically charge their best customers.

Principal The principal is the amount borrowed on credit and excludes interest or other charges.

Probability of Default (PD) The probability of default is the likelihood that a loan will not be repaid.

Provision for loan loss A provision for loan loss is recorded on the income statement. It represents funds set aside to absorb anticipated loan losses.

Public borrower A public borrower is typically a sovereign state, or a regional, provincial, municipal, or local government, or a non-independent agency affiliated with such borrowers.

Recovery rate (RR) The recovery rate is the fraction of a defaulted obligation that can be recovered.

Regulatory capital requirement A regulatory capital requirement specifies how much minimum capital a bank must hold to guard against the various risks it takes, such as credit risk, market risk, and operational risk.

Repurchase agreement or repo A repurchase agreement, "repo," is a contract between two parties in which one party sells the other a security at a specified price with the obligation to buy the security bank at a later date for another specified price. They are widely used by central banks to provide support to meet banks' short-term liquidity needs.

Retail bank Retail banks primarily service individuals, or consumers, and small and medium-sized enterprises (SMEs).

Retail borrower A retail borrower is an individual who borrows money to purchase a home, car, and other goods and services.

Risk appetite Risk appetite is the level of risk exposure an investor is willing to assume in exchange for the potential for a profit.

Risk management Risk management is a structured approach to monitoring, measuring, and managing exposures to reduce the potential impact of an uncertain event.

Risk policy A risk policy outlines the risk management framework of an organization in relationship to its objectives, and varies across and within industries and companies based on the organization's ability to absorb losses and the rate of return it seeks from its operations.

Risk transfer Risk transfer is the assumption of a specific risk for a fee or premium.

Risk-weighted assets Risk-weighted assets equal the sum of various financial assets multiplied by their respective risk weights and off-balance-sheet items weighted for their credit risk according to the regulatory requirements outlined by banking regulators and supervisors.

Scenario analysis Scenario analysis, or "what-if" analysis, assesses the potential outcome of various scenarios by setting up several possible situations and analyzing the potential outcomes of each situation.

Seasonal financing A seasonal loan finances a temporary and predictable short-term demand, such as seasonal increases in inventory or farm-related financing.

Securitization Securitization is a process where illiquid cash-flow-producing assets (such as mortgages, credit cards, and loans, etc.) are pooled into a portfolio. The purchase of these assets for the portfolio is financed by securities issued to investors who then share the cash flows generated by the portfolio.

Security A (financial) security is a fungible financial instrument.

Senior debt Senior debt has priority over all other more junior and subordinated debt in case of bankruptcy, default, or similar events.

Settlement risk Settlement risk (also known as "Herstatt" risk) is the risk that a counterparty fails to perform as agreed and does not deliver a security or its value after the other counterparty has already delivered on the same transaction. (The failure of Herstatt Bank in 1974 exposed many investors to this type of risk.)

Shareholder A shareholder (stockholder or equity holder) is one of the owners of a corporation, has the right to elect the board of directors, may decide in corporate matters, and may receive dividends.

Shareholders' equity Shareholders' equity is calculated as the difference between assets and liabilities and is the shareholders' investment in the company, which typically equals the amount the shareholders have directly invested in the company as well as the company's retained earnings.

Short position A short position, the opposite of a long position, represents either the selling of a borrowed asset, writing of an option, or selling of a futures position. When the asset's value increases, the position's value decreases and when the asset's value decreases, the position's value increases.

Short-term lending Short-term lending has a maturity of less than one year and finances temporary requirements and seasonal needs.

Small and Medium-Sized Enterprises (SME) Small and medium-sized enterprises are usually partnerships, proprietorships, owner-operated companies, or other types of small business or corporation whose sales, assets, operations, and headcount falls below a certain limit.

Solvency Solvency denotes the financial condition of a company or financial institution when assets exceed liabilities.

Sovereign credit Sovereign credit is direct borrowing by, or a borrowing guaranteed by, the government of a sovereign state.

Sovereign credit risk Sovereign credit risk is the risk that a sovereign state or government will default on or delay the repayment of its debts.

Specific, non-systematic, unique risk Specific, non-systematic, unique risk is the risk of an adverse movement in the price of one individual security or financial asset due to factors specific to that particular security or issuer.

Speculation Speculation involves the buying (long position), holding, selling, and short selling (short position) of financial assets, commodities, foreign exchange, or derivatives in the expectation that price fluctuations will generate a profit. It also refers to a position that is not hedged, or simply the buying or selling of an asset with the hope of earning a profit.

Standardized Approach The Standardized Approach to calculate a bank's credit and market risk capital is the simplest approach outlined in the Basel II Accord.

Strategic risk Strategic risk is the potential loss due to poor business decisions or execution.

Stress testing Stress testing assesses the potential outcome of specific changes that are fundamental, material, and adverse.

Swap A swap is a derivative that allows two counterparties to exchange streams of future cash flows with each other.

Systemic risk Systemic risk is the risk of a system-wide breakdown in the banking or financial system.

Temporary financing Temporary financing provides capital through short- or medium-term debt. It includes seasonal and cyclical loans.

Through-The-Cycle (TTC) model The Through-The-Cycle model determines regulatory capital adequacy to reflect the risk and the associated regulatory capital requirements throughout the credit and business cycle.

Tier 1 capital Tier 1 capital in the Basel Accords is the core capital of a bank and refers to equity capital and to certain types of disclosed reserves as well as particular debt/equity hybrid securities.

Tier 2 capital Tier 2 capital in the Basel Accords is supplementary capital and refers to undisclosed and certain disclosed reserves, general provisions, general loan loss reserves, hybrid capital instruments, and subordinated debt.

Trading book The trading book of a bank is the portfolio of various positions in financial assets, instruments, and commodities that a bank holds with the intention to trade or to hedge other positions in the trading book.

Uncommitted facility An uncommitted facility is a loan with loosely specified terms and conditions but with an understanding, but not an obligation, that the funds will be made available by the lender upon demand.

Underwriting Underwriting assesses a borrower's eligibility to receive a credit, a loan, or a bond by analyzing financial and other information about the potential borrower.

Unexpected loss Unexpected loss describes the loss in excess of the expected loss and is expressed at a certain statistical confidence level.

Value-at-Risk (VaR) Value-at-Risk is a measure of risk that estimates the potential loss of a portfolio of financial assets.

Index